4413130500

Operations Management

Second Edition

Nigel Slack, Stuart Chambers, Christine Harland, Alan Harrison, Robert Johnston

INSTRUCTOR'S MANUAL

by
Andy Neely
University of Cambridge

Note: The material in this Manual may be reproduced
for OHP transparencies and student handouts, without the express
permission of the Publishers, for educational purposes only.

FINANCIAL TIMES
PITMAN PUBLISHING

LONDON · HONG KONG · JOHANNESBURG
MELBOURNE · SINGAPORE · WASHINGTON DC

FINANCIAL TIMES MANAGEMENT
128 Long Acre, London WC2E 9AN
Tel: +44 (0)171 447 2000
Fax: +44 (0)171 240 5771
Website: www.ftmanagement.com

A Division of Financial Times Professional Limited

Instructor's Manual first published in Great Britain in 1995
Second edition of the Manual published in Great Britain in 1998

Instructor's Manual © 1995, 1998 Andrew Neely
based on material in *Operations Management 1e & 2e*
© Nigel Slack, Stuart Chambers, Christine Harland,
Alan Harrison and Robert Johnston 1995, 1998

ISBN 0 273 62689 2

British Library Cataloguing in Publication Data
A CIP catalogue record for this book can be obtained from the British Library

All rights reserved. Permission is hereby given for the material
in this publication to be reproduced for OHP transparencies and
student handouts, without the express permission of the Publishers,
for educational purposes only. In all other cases, no part of this
publication may be reproduced, stored in a retrieval system, or
transmitted in any form or by any means, electronic, mechanical,
photocopying, recording, or otherwise without either the prior
written permission of the Publishers or a licence permitting restricted
copying in the United Kingdom issued by the Copyright Licensing
Agency Ltd, 90 Tottenham Court Road, London W1P 0LP. This
publication may not be lent, resold, hired out or otherwise disposed
of by way of trade in any form of binding or cover other than that in
which it is published, without the prior consent of the Publishers.

10 9 8 7 6 5 4 3 2 1

Printed by Bell and Bain Ltd, Glasgow

The Publishers' policy is to use paper manufactured from sustainable forests.

Contents

Preface

This instructor's manual has been written with two aims in mind. First, it is designed to make the second edition of *Operations Management* a 'lecturer-friendly' textbook. Second, it is copyright free and can therefore be circulated to students as additional course material.

The instructor's manual consists of the same twenty-one chapters as the second edition of *Operations Management*. Each chapter has been laid out in a common format.

The first part of each chapter:

- identifies the key questions addressed in that chapter;

- lists the topics covered in that chapter;

- summarises the main points made in that chapter.

The remainder of the chapter uses a series of 'double-page spreads' to:

- identify key points to make about the topic being covered;

- provide a master slide which can be used to make these key points.

The instructor's manual is not meant to be exhaustive. If you decide to use it you will almost certainly want to supplement it with additional materials. Having said this, I hope those of you who adopt the second edition of *Operations Management* as a course text find this manual valuable and would welcome any comments you have on how it might be improved.

Andy Neely
Cambridge
February 1998

Acknowledgements

The concepts and ideas contained in this instructor's manual draw on many different sources. For a full list of acknowledgements and references the reader is referred to the second edition of *Operations Management*.

CHAPTER 1

OPERATIONS MANAGEMENT

Key questions
• What is operations management?
• What are the similarities between all operations?
• How are operations different from each other?
• What do operations managers do?

Topics covered
• The part which operations management plays in organizations.
• The position of the operations function in the structure of an organization.
• How the input-transformation-output model can be used to describe all types of operation no matter what they produce.
• The concepts of macro and micro operations and internal customer-supplier relationships.
• How operations buffer themselves against environmental uncertainty.
• The many different types of operation and how they can be categorized on four dimensions.
• The activities of operations managers.

Summary

What is operations management?
• Operations management is the term which is used for the activities, decisions and responsibilities of operations managers who manage the arrangement of resources which are devoted to the production of goods and services within an organization.
• It is one of the major functions of any business though it may not be called operations management in some industries.
• The span of responsibility varies between companies. Some have narrow definitions of the operations function which encompass only the core direct activities which are concerned with the production of goods and services. Others take a broader definition of the function to include all direct and indirect supporting activities within the organization.
• Operations management can also be viewed as that part of any function's or manager's responsibility which involves producing the internal goods and services within an organization, as opposed to the strictly technical decisions which they take within their functions.

What are the similarities between all operations?
• All operations can be modelled as an input-transformation-output system.
• All have inputs of transforming resources which are usually divided into 'facilities' and 'staff'. All have also transformed resources which are some mixture of materials, information and customers.
• All operations transform inputs into outputs by acting on some aspect of their physical properties, informational properties, possession, location, physiological state or psychological state.
• All operations produce some mixture of tangible goods or products and less tangible services. Few operations produce only products or only services.
• All operations can be divided into micro operations which form a network of internal customer-supplier relationships within the operation.
• All operations can be viewed as a set of business processes which often cut across functionally based micro operations.

How are operations different from each other?

• Operations differ in terms of the volumes of their outputs, from low volume to high volume. High volume is usually associated with lower cost.

• All operations vary in terms of the variation in demand with which they have to cope. Low variation is usually associated with low cost.

• All operations vary in terms of the degree of customer contact which they have. This is the amount of value-adding activity which takes place with the customer present. Low customer contact is usually associated with low cost.

What do operations managers do?

• They translate the strategic direction of an organization into operational action.

• They design the operation; this means not only the design of the products and the services themselves but the system or processes which produce them.

• They plan and control the activities of the operation by deciding when and where activities will take place and detecting and responding to any deviations from plan.

• They improve the performance of the operation with reference to its strategic objectives through some combination of major and minor improvement activities.

What is operations management?

Points to make

1 **Operations management is about the way organizations produce goods and services.**

Operations managers organize the production and delivery of the goods and services we all use. Such goods and services include what we eat, what we sit on, what we read, what we listen to and even what we play with.

2 **To understand operations management we need to understand:**
- that the operations function is 'the arrangement of resources which are devoted to the production of goods and services';

- that an operations manager is 'a member of the organization who has responsibility for managing some, or all, of the resources that comprise the operations function';

- that operations management is 'the term used to describe the activities, decisions and responsibilities of an operations manager'.

3 **Operations management involves both today and tomorrow.**

Operations managers have to ensure that resources are used efficiently so that today's customers can be satisfied and today's competitors can be beaten.

Operations managers also have to find ways of using resources more efficiently so that tomorrow's customers can be satisfied and tomorrow's competitors can be beaten.

What is operations management?

- Operations management is about the way organizations produce goods and services.

- To understand operations management we need to understand:

    - what the operations function constitutes;

    - what the operations manager does.

- Operations management involves both today and tomorrow.

The position of the operations function in the organization

Points to make

1   Most organizations consist of two types of function:
- major functions such as operations, marketing, accounting and finance, product and/or service development;

- support functions such as human resources, purchasing, engineering.

2   The boundaries between these functions vary from organization to organization.

Depending on the organizations the operations function might be responsible for developing products and/or services, choosing process technologies, devising delivery schedules, buying in materials, buying in services, devising budgets, recruiting and training staff.

3   The functional structure of organizations is a human creation.

An alternative is to look at processes and explore the organization in terms of the flows of information and materials within it.

The position of the operations function

	Marketing	Accounting and finance	Product development	Operations
Church	Call on newcomers	Manage appeals	Retranslate scriptures	Conduct weddings
Fast food chain	Advertise on television	Pay suppliers	Design hamburgers	Make hamburgers
Furniture manufacturer	Sell to stores	Pay staff	Design new furniture	Assemble furniture

Process perspective	Identify needs	Raise capital	Develop product	Make and distribute

OHP2

The input-transformation-output model of operations

Points to make

1   Operations produce goods and/or services.

The output of an operation can usually be classified on a spectrum ranging from pure goods to pure services. Most operations produce either goods which are accompanied by facilitating services, or services which are accompanied by facilitating goods.

2   All goods and services are produced via a transformation process.

Operations take inputs, transform them, or use them to transform something else, thereby producing outputs which are of a higher value than the inputs.

3   At a macro level all operations conform to this input-transformation-output model. At a micro level differences can be observed.

Depending on the operation the inputs can be either transforming or transformed resources. Transforming resources include facilities and staff. Transformed resources include materials, information and customers.

The transformation process varies depending on the transformed resource. If the transformed resource is materials then the transformation process might be concerned with physical properties, location (parcel delivery), or possession (retail store). If the transformed resource is information then the transformation process might be concerned with informational properties (accounting), possession (market research), store (library), or location (telecommunications). If the transformed resource is a customer then the transformation process might be concerned with physical properties (cosmetic surgeon), store (hotel), location (airline), physiological state (hospital), or psychological state (theatre).

The outputs of operations also differ in terms of their:

- Tangibility - can you physically touch the product or service? Goods are usually tangible; services are not.

- Storability - can you store the product or service? Goods can usually be stored; services cannot.

- Transportability - can you transport the product or service from one location to another? Goods can usually be transported; services cannot.

- Simultaneity - when are the products and/or services produced? Goods are usually produced prior to the customer receiving them. Services are often produced simultaneously to their consumption.

- Customer contact - customers usually have low contact with organizations producing goods and high contact with those providing services.

- Quality - how do customers judge the quality of the goods or services they receive? As customers do not normally see goods being produced, they will tend to judge the quality of an operation producing goods by the quality of the goods themselves. As customers are intimately involved in the provision of a service, they will tend to judge the quality of an operation providing services by looking at both the actual service and the way in which it is delivered.

The input-transformation-output model

Transformed resources

| Materials |
| Information |
| Customers |

Input

Transforming resources

| Facilities |
| Staff |

Transformation process

Output

Goods and services

Macro and micro operations

Points to make

1   The input-transformation-output model can be used to describe macro and micro operations.

All operations consist of micro operations, each of which produces outputs by taking inputs and transforming them, or using them to transform something else. This input-transformation-output model can be extended to the level of the individual.

2   There are two important implications of this model.

First, the input-transformation-output model makes explicit the fact that other parts of the organization can be viewed as 'operations' and hence some of the tools and techniques of operations management might be useful elsewhere in the organization.

Second, the input-transformation-output model underpins the concept of the internal customer-supplier.

3   Organizations are networks of internal customers and suppliers.

Each micro operation is a customer of, and a supplier to, another micro operation. Hence the organization as a whole consists of a network of internal customers and suppliers.

4   A caveat - internal customer-supplier relationships are not the same as external customer-supplier relationships.

Internal customers and suppliers do not operate in a free market.

5   The connections between micro operations are business processes.

Each micro operation makes a contribution to satisfying customer needs. These various contributions come together in the form of business processes, which address the core purposes of the operation and often cut across conventional organizational boundaries.

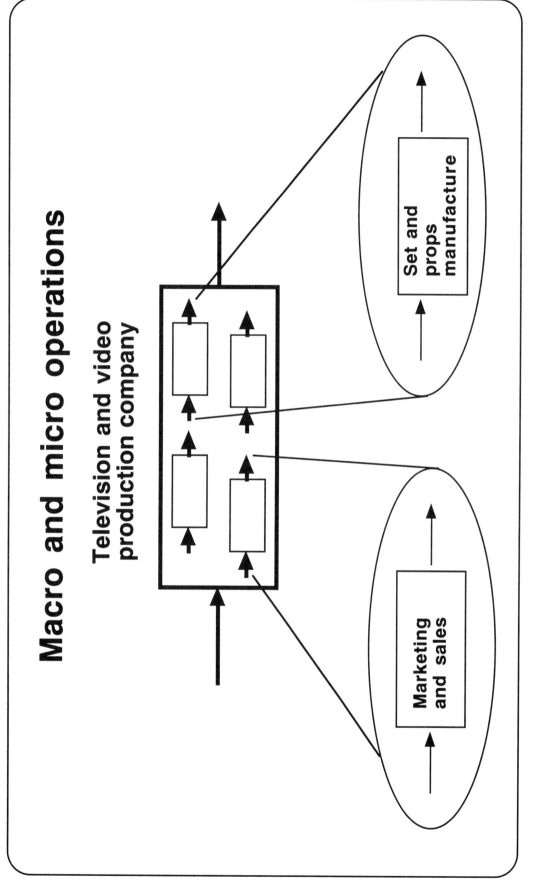

Macro and micro operations

Television and video
production company

Marketing
and sales

Set and
props
manufacture

Buffering the operation against environmental uncertainty

Points to make

1   The operations function exists in a turbulent environment.
For operations to be efficient stability is required. Hence the operations function has to be buffered against environmental uncertainty.

2   Operations can be buffered in two ways:
- Through physical buffering - keeping an inventory or stock of resources either at the input or the output side of the transformation process.

- Through organizational buffering - allocating responsibility so that the operations function is protected from the external environment by the other functions.

3   Traditionally buffering was thought appropriate.   Now it is criticised for the following reasons:
The time lag of communicating between the insulating function and operations function makes change difficult. By the time the insulating function has responded, operations has moved on to the next problem.

Operations never develops the understanding of the environment which would help it exploit new developments.

Operations is never required to take responsibility for its actions. There is always another function to blame and unhelpful conflict may arise between functions.

Physical buffering often involves tolerating large stocks of input or output resources which are both expensive and prevent operations improving.

Physical buffering in customer processing operations means making the customer wait for the service, which could lead to customer dissatisfaction.

4   Today the trend is towards exposing the operations function to environmental turbulence.

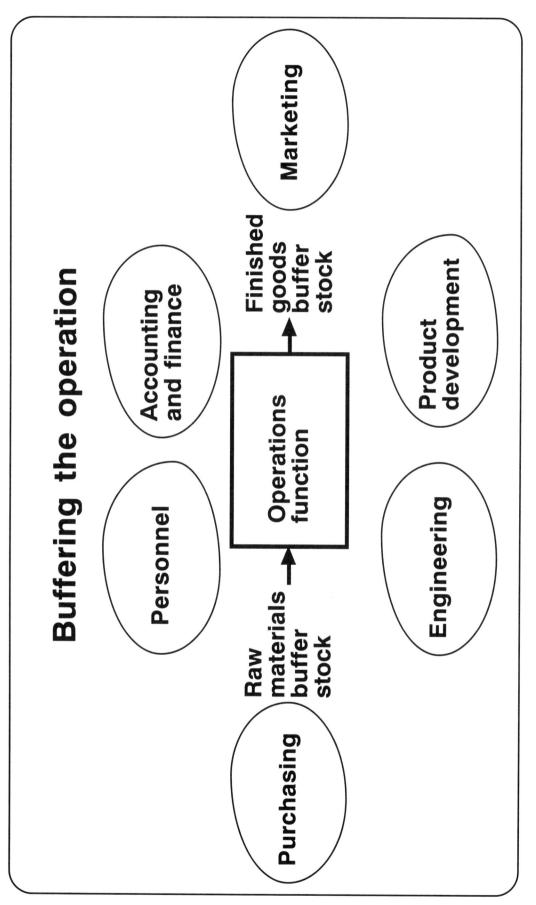

Buffering the operation

Purchasing

Personnel

Accounting and finance

Marketing

Raw materials buffer stock

Operations function

Finished goods buffer stock

Engineering

Product development

OHP5

The many different types of operation

Points to make

1 An operation can be categorized using four dimensions.
These are output volume, output variety, variation in demand and degree of customer contact.

2 High output volumes result in operations which:
- involve highly repetitive tasks;

- are easy to specialize;

- are easy to systemize;

- are highly capital intensive;

- have low unit costs.

3 High output variety results in operations which:
- need to be flexible;

- are complex;

- provide a service which has to be closely matched to customer needs;

- have high unit costs.

4 High variation in demand results in operations which:
- need to be flexible;

- have to anticipate future demand;

- have to be able to change their capacity.

5 High customer contact results in operations which:
- need to be able to offer fast service as waiting tolerance is likely to be low;

- use customer perception to measure performance;

- need skilled staff.

6 Often operations with high customer contact have back-office as well as front-office jobs.
Back-office jobs are those that are done behind the scenes. They involve little direct customer contact.

7 The positioning of the operation has implications for the cost of creation products and services.
High volume, low variety, low variation and low customer contact all help to keep processing costs low.

A typology of operations

	Low — Volume — High	
Low repetition Staff members perform more of job Less systemization High unit costs		High repeatability Specialization Systemization Capital intensive Low unit costs
	High — Variety — Low	
Flexible Complex Match customer needs High unit cost		Well defined Routine Standardized Low unit costs
	High — Variation in demand — Low	
Changing capacity Anticipation Flexibility In touch with demand High unit cost		Stable Routine Predictable High utilization Low unit cost
	High — Customer contact — Low	
Short waiting tolerance Satisfaction governed by perception Customer contact skills High unit cost		Time lag between production and consumption High staff utilization Low unit cost

The activities of operations managers

Points to make

1 **The activities of operations managers fall into two categories.**
These are those the operations manager has indirect responsibility for and those the operations manager has direct responsibility for.

2 **Activities which operations managers may have indirect responsibility for include:**

- informing other functions of the opportunities and constraints provided by the operation's capabilities;

- discussing with other functions how operations plans and their own plans might be modified to the benefit of both functions.

- encouraging other functions to suggest ways in which the operations function can improve the service it provides to the rest of the organization.

3 **Activities which operations managers may have direct responsibility for include:**
Understanding operations strategic objectives. This involves:

- developing a clear vision which explains how the operations function can help the organization achieve its long-term goals;

- translating these goals into explicit performance objectives for operations.

Developing an operations strategy. Operations management involves hundreds of minute-by-minute decisions. Operations managers need guiding principles which will help them consistently make appropriate decisions. A good operations strategy should provide such guiding principles.

Designing the organization's products, processes and services. Sometimes operations managers are responsible only for designing the processes. Sometimes they are responsible for designing the products, processes and services.

Planning and controlling the operation. The operations function has limited resources. Operations managers need to plan and control the use of these resources, through activities such as inventory and capacity management.

Improving the performance of the operation. Operations management not only involves doing things right today. It also involves working out how things can be done better tomorrow - a process which is continuous.

The activities of operations managers

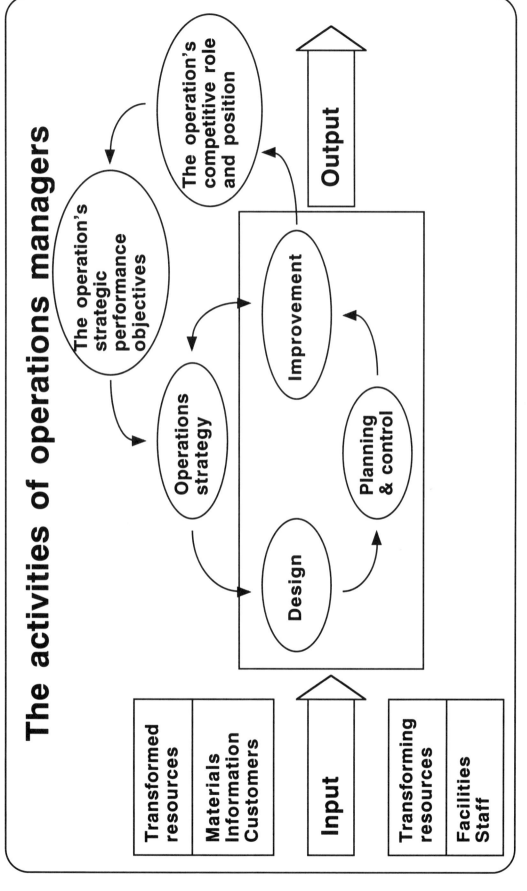

OHP7

CHAPTER 2

THE STRATEGIC ROLE AND OBJECTIVES OF OPERATIONS

Key questions
• What role and contribution should the operations function play in achieving strategic success?
• What are the performance objectives of operations and what are the internal and external benefits which derive from excelling in each of them?

Topics covered
• The role of the operations function in the organization's strategic plans.
• How the contribution of the operations function to the organization's competitiveness can be assessed.
• The meaning of the operations function's five performance objectives - quality, speed, dependability, flexibility and cost.
• The internal and external benefits which an operation can derive from excelling in each of its objectives.

Summary
What role and contribution should the operations function play in achieving strategic success?
• Any operations function has three main roles to play within an organization:
    - as an implementor of the organization's strategies.
    - as a supporter of the organization's overall strategy.
    - as a leader of strategy.
• The extent to which the operations function fulfils these roles together with its aspirations can be used to judge the operations function's contribution to the organization. Hayes and Wheelwright provide a four-stage model for doing this.

What are the performance objectives of operations and what are the internal and external benefits which derive from excelling in each of them?
• By 'doing things right' the operations function seeks to influence the quality of the organization's goods and services. Externally quality is an important aspect of customer satisfaction or dissatisfaction. Internally quality operations both reduce costs and increase dependability.
• By 'doing things fast' the operations function seeks to influence the speed with which goods and services are delivered. Externally speed is an important aspect of customer service. Internally speed both reduces inventories by decreasing internal throughput time and reduces risks by delaying the commitment of resources.
• By 'doing things on time' the operations function seeks to influence the dependability of the delivery of goods and services. Externally dependability is an important aspect of customer service. Internally dependability within operations increases operational reliability thus saving the time and money that would otherwise be taken up in solving reliability problems and also giving stability to the operation.

• By 'changing what they do' the operations function seeks to influence the flexibility with which the organization produces goods and services. Externally flexibility can:
  - produce new products and services (product/service flexibility)
  - produce a wide range or mix of products and services (mix flexibility)
  - produce different quantities or volumes of products and services (volume flexibility)
  - produce products and services at different times (delivery flexibility)

Internally flexibility can help speed up response times, save time wasted in changeovers and maintain dependability

• By 'doing things cheaply' the operations function seeks to influence the cost of the organization's goods and services. Externally low costs allow organisations to reduce their price in order to gain higher volumes or alternatively increase their profitability on existing volume levels. Internally cost performance is helped by good performance in the other performance objectives.

The role of the operations function

Points to make

1   The principal role of operations is to produce the goods and services demanded by the organization's customers.
But this is not all an operations function does.

2   Operations must help implement the business strategy.
Strategy is intangible. It starts life as a statement of intent and only comes into being as decisions are made and actions are taken. The operations function often holds the majority of a firm's resources. For a strategy to be implemented these resources have to be deployed in a consistent manner over an extended period of time.

3   Operations must support the business strategy.
Operations must make sure that its resources provide the capabilities the organization needs to achieve its strategic objectives. This means that everything about the operation (its technology, staff, systems and procedures) must be appropriate.

4   Operations should seek to drive the business strategy.
If the operations function cannot make high quality products, or fails to keep its delivery promises, the business will die. Alternatively if the operations function does things well it can provide a source of competitive advantage.

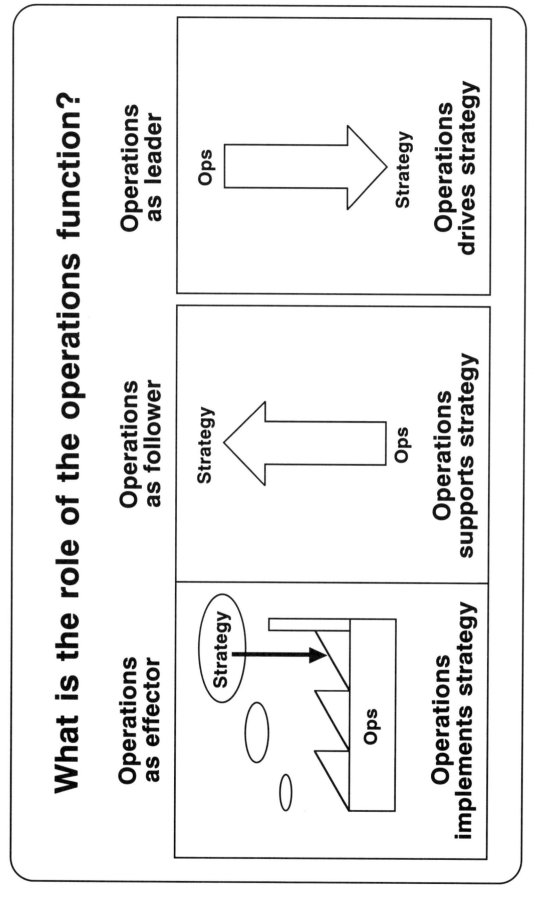

What is the role of the operations function?

Operations as effector

Operations implements strategy

Operations as follower

Operations supports strategy

Operations as leader

Operations drives strategy

OHP8

How the contribution of operations can be assessed

Points to make

1 **Professors Hayes and Wheelwright, of Harvard Business School, provide a useful model for assessing the contribution of the operations function.**
   This model can be used in two ways. First, members of the operations function can be asked what their aspirations are. Second, members of other functions can be asked how they see operations.

2 **Hayes and Wheelwright's model describes the four stages of operations strategic development.**

3 **For stage 1 firms, the objective is to minimize the negative impact of operations.**
   In stage 1 firms:
   • external 'experts' will be used to make decisions of strategic importance to operations.

   • internal management control systems will be used to monitor operations performance.

   • operations will be encouraged to be flexible and reactive.

4 **For stage 2 firms, the objective is for operations to help the business maintain parity with its competitors.**
   In stage 2 firms:
   • industry practice will be followed.

   • the planning horizon for operations investment will be extended so that it incorporates a single business cycle.

   • capital investment will be seen primarily as a way of catching up with the competition.

5 **For stage 3 firms, the objective is for operations to provide credible support for the business strategy.**
   In stage 3 firms:
   • operations investments will be screened for consistency with the business strategy.

   • the implications for operations of changes in business strategy will be considered.

   • a systematic approach to the long-term development of the operations function will be adopted.

6 **For stage 4 firms, the objective is for operations to provide a source of competitive advantage.**
   In stage 4 firms:
   • efforts will be made to anticipate the potential of new operations practices and technologies.

   • operations will be involved in major marketing and engineering decisions.

   • long-range programmes will be pursued in order to acquire capabilities in advance of needs.

How can the contribution of the operations function be assessed?

	Neutral	Supportive
Internally	**Stage 1** Objective is to minimize the negative impact of 'operations'.	**Stage 3** Objective is for 'operations' to provide credible support for the business strategy.
Externally	**Stage 2** Objective is for 'operations' to help the business maintain parity with its competitors.	**Stage 4** Objective is for 'operations' to provide a source of competitive advantage.

The meaning of the five performance objectives

Points to make

1 Operations has five performance objectives.

2 Quality - doing things right.
Doing things right means not making mistakes. It involves providing error-free goods and services which are fit for their purpose.

In many operations quality is the most visible performance objective as it is relatively easy for customers to judge.

3 Speed - doing things fast.
Doing things fast involves minimizing the time between the customer asking for and receiving the goods or services.

Speed affects the availability of goods and services. The faster an organization can deliver a particular product or service the less likely a customer is to go elsewhere.

4 Dependability - doing things on time.
Doing things on time involves keeping delivery promises. Customers can only judge an organization's dependability once they have purchased something from that organization. Hence dependability affects the customers re-purchase decision.

To be dependable organizations must be able to:
- estimate delivery dates accurately;

- communicate them to the customer;

- deliver when promised.

5 Flexibility - being able to change what you do.
Being able to change what you do involves being able to adapt the operation's activities. The advantage of flexibility is that it helps organizations cope with unexpected circumstances.

There are two dimensions to flexibility: being able to change fast enough and being able to change far enough.

There are also a number of different types of flexibility:
- product/service flexibility - being able to offer a wide range of products and services.

- mix flexibility - being able to change the mix of products and services offered.

- volume flexibility - being able to change the volume of product made.

- delivery flexibility - being able to cope with changing customer demands in terms of due dates.

6 Cost - doing things cheaply.
Doing things cheaply involves getting the right mix of staff, facilities and materials.

Everyone wants low cost. In many ways cost is the most important performance objective.

What do the terms quality, speed, dependability, flexibility and cost mean in the context of operations?

Which enables you to do things cheaply (cost advantage)?

Which enables you to change what you do (flexibility advantage)?

Which enables you to do things quickly (speed advantage)?

Enables you to do things on time (dependability advantage)?

Being able to do things right (quality advantage)?

OHP10

The benefits of excelling at the performance objectives

Points to make

1   There are external and internal benefits of excelling at the five performance objectives.
The external benefits come from enhanced customer satisfaction. The internal benefits come from increased stability and efficiency.

2   Quality - doing things right.
Externally - quality means you do not make mistakes. You provide 'error-free' products and services which are 'fit for their purpose'.

Internally - quality reduces costs and increases dependability. Doing things right means you do not have to spend time (and money) rectifying mistakes.

3   Speed - doing things fast.
Externally - speed means you get your products and services to your customers fast, thus increasing their availability.

Internally - speed reduces inventories and risks. Doing things fast means that materials flow through your organization quickly, thus eliminating queues and reducing any risk of obsolescence.

4   Dependability - doing things on time.
Externally - dependability means you do what you promised. You deliver your products and services on time, thus meeting your commitments.

Internally - dependability saves money, time and provides stability. Disruptions often cost money and waste time. Doing things when promised minimises the risk of such disruption.

5   Flexibility - being able to change what you do.
Externally - flexibility means that you are able to change what you do, both far enough (range) and fast enough (response). Being flexible means you can cope with changing circumstances or demands.

Internally - flexibility speeds up response, saves time and maintains dependability. Changing demands always cause problems. Being flexible means that you are able to absorb some of these easily.

6   Cost - doing things cheaply.
Externally - doing things cheaply means you can offer your product or service to the market at a price it will bear, while still achieving a return for your business.

Internally - quality operations do not waste time or effort having to re-do things nor are their internal customers inconvenienced by flawed service. Hence high quality can mean low costs. Fast operations reduce the level of in-process inventory between micro operations as well as reducing administrative overheads. Both effects can reduce the overall cost of the operation. Dependable operations do not spring any unwelcome surprises on their internal customers. They can be relied on to deliver exactly as planned. This eliminates wasteful disruption and allows the other micro operations to operate efficiently. Flexible operations adapt to changing circumstances quickly and without disrupting the rest of the operation. Also flexible micro operations can change over between tasks quickly and without wasting time and capacity.

The benefits of excelling

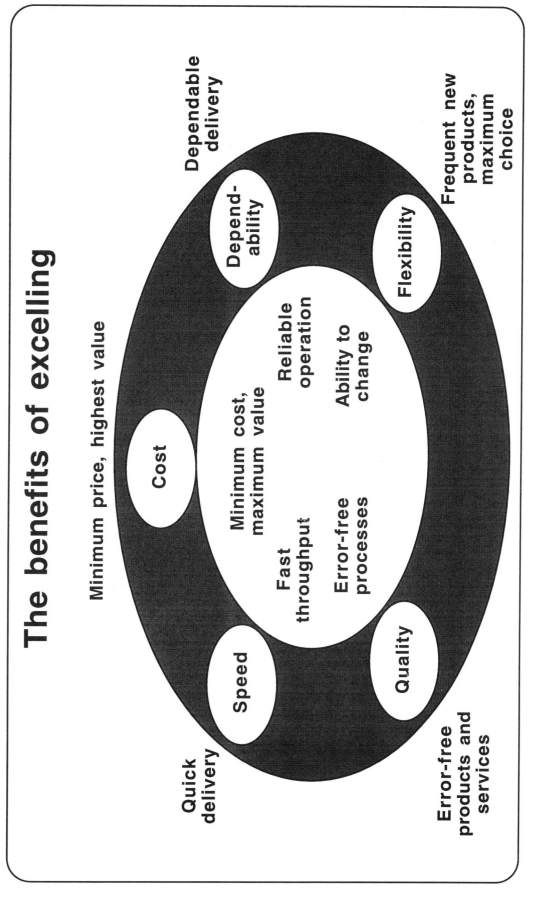

Minimum price, highest value

Dependable delivery

Frequent new products, maximum choice

Quick delivery

Error-free products and services

Dependability

Flexibility

Cost

Speed

Quality

Minimum cost, maximum value

Reliable operation

Fast throughput

Error-free processes

Ability to change

CHAPTER 3

OPERATIONS STRATEGY

Key questions
• What is an operations strategy?
• How does operations strategy fit into a company's overall strategy?
• How do we know which performance objectives are the most important?
• What are the specific decision areas which are usually included in an operations strategy?
• How can an operations strategy be put together?

Topics covered
• The strategy hierarchy of which operations strategy is a part.
• The nature and content of operations strategy.
• How performance objectives will have different priorities depending upon the organization's customers, competitors and the position of its products and services on their life cycle.
• The operations strategy decision areas.
• The impact of the operations strategy decision areas on the performance objectives.
• The formulation of operations strategy.

Summary
What is an operations strategy?
• Operations strategy is the total pattern of decisions and actions which set the role, objectives and activities of the operation so that they contribute to and support the organization's business strategy. This definition refers to the macro operation, but one can also use the term 'operations strategy' which identifies how the micro operation is going to contribute to the operations strategy of the whole business.
• An operations strategy has *content* and *process*. The *content* of an operations strategy deals with the relative importance of the performance objectives to the operation as well as with giving general guidance to decision-making activities within the operation. The *process* of the operations strategy is the procedure which is used within the operation to formulate the operations strategy.

How does operations strategy fit into a company's overall strategy?
• Strategic decisions can be viewed at a number of levels. *Corporate strategy* sets the objectives for the different businesses which make up a group of businesses. *Business strategy* sets the objectives for each individual business and how it positions itself in the market place. *Functional strategies* set the objectives for each function's contribution to its business strategy. In this sense we use the term operations strategy as a functional strategy which deals with the parts of the organization which create goods and services.
• It is common to define any level of strategy in a similar way to that in which we defined operations strategy. So the strategy of any organization or part of an organization is the total pattern of decisions and actions which position the organization in its environment.

How do we know which performance objectives are the most important?
• The relative importance to an operation of performance objectives is influenced by the organization's specific customer groups and their needs, the activities of the organization's competitors, and the stage of its products and services in their life cycle. A particularly important concept here is the distinction between order-winning performance objectives and order-qualifying performance objectives. This distinction is used in some operations strategy formulation processes (for example, the Hill methodology).

What are the specific decision areas which are usually included in an operations strategy?

• Strategic decision areas in operations are usually divided into *structural* and *infrastructural* decisions. Structural decisions are those which define an operations shape and form. What, in the rest of the book, we call design activities are largely structural decisions. Infrastructural decisions are those which influence the systems and procedures which determine how the operation will work in practice. Workforce organization, planning and control and improvement activities are infrastructural decisions.

How can an operations strategy be put together?

• There are many different procedures which are used by companies, consultancies and academics to formulate operations strategies. The two we describe in this chapter are the Hill methodology and the Platts-Gregory procedure. The Hill methodology is based on the idea of making connections between different levels of strategy-making from corporate objectives through marketing strategy, operations objectives and structural and infrastructural decisions. The Platts-Gregory procedure is based on identifying the gaps between, on the one hand what the market requires from an operation and on the other, how the operation is performing against market requirements.

The strategy hierarchy of which operations strategy is a part

Points to make

1   Strategy involves commitment to action.

Strategies commit organizations to particular courses of action. They define what the organization is going to do, and, by implication, what it is not going to do.

2   Not all commitments to action are strategic.

Strategic commitments are those which: (a) have widespread effect; (b) are significant; (c) define the position of the organization relative to its environment; and (d) move the organization closer to its long-term goals.

3   Strategies provide general guidelines.

Strategies provide general guidelines, which, if followed, ensure that future decisions and actions move the organization towards its goals.

4   The scope of a strategy depends on the organization being considered.

If 'the organization' is a large diversified corporation, its strategy will define where it positions itself in its global, economic, political and social environment and will consist of decisions about what type of business the group wants to be in, what parts of the world it wants to operate in, what businesses to acquire and what to divest, how to allocate cash between its various businesses and so on. Decisions such as these form the corporate strategy.

If 'the organization' is a business unit within a corporate group it will need to put together a business strategy which sets out its individual mission and objectives as well as defining how it intends to compete in its markets. This business strategy guides the business in an environment which consists of its customers, markets and competitors, but also includes the corporate group of which it is a part.

Similarly within a business each function will need to consider what part it should play in contributing to the strategic and/or competitive objectives of the business. The operations, marketing, finance and R&D, and other functions will all need to translate the business objectives into terms which have meaning for them and consider how best they should organize their resources to support them. In other words each function of the business needs a functional strategy which guides its actions within the business. This time the 'environment' of the function includes the business itself.

The key point is that different types of 'organization' have to make different types of decision, which, in turn, will be influenced by different things.

5   The hierarchical model is an over-simplification.

Strategies are not formed in a purely top-down fashion. They can evolve, for example, as new technologies or market opportunities emerge. Thus a business strategy, or even a functional strategy, can influence a corporate strategy.

6   The hierarchical model can be extended to operations.

Within the 'macro' operations function, there are a whole host of 'micro operations', each of which may need a strategy to guide its decision and actions.

The strategy hierarchy

Key strategic decisions

Influences on decision making

Corporate strategy

What business to be in?
What to acquire?
What to divest?
How to allocate cash?

Economic environment
Social environment
Political environment
Company values and ethics

Business strategy

What is the mission?
What are the strategic objectives of the firm?
How to compete?

Customer/market dynamics
Competitor activity
Core technology dynamics
Financial constraints

Functional strategy

How to contribute to the strategic objectives?
How to manage the function's resources?

Skills of function's staff
Current technology
Recent performance of the function

OHP12

The nature and content of operations strategy

Points to make

1   Operations strategy has two dimensions: process and content.
Content explores what the strategy should contain - the collection of policies, plans and behaviour the operation chooses to pursue. Process explores how the strategy should be developed - the way in which the policies, plans and behaviour are decided.

2   Content splits into performance objectives and policy decisions.
The performance objectives specify what the organization wants to be good at.

The policy decision areas specify how the organization will seek to achieve the level of performance it desires.

For example, if an organization wants to be good at meeting its delivery promises (a performance objective), it might choose to increase the number of lorries it has in its fleet, or set up regional distribution depots (policy decisions).

3   The performance objectives should be prioritized.
If you ask people what their organization wants, or needs, to be good at, they are likely to say something along the lines of 'we need to be able to deliver quality goods, at the right price, in the right quantity, to the right place, at the right time' - i.e. they will want to be good at everything. Unfortunately it is not always possible to do all of these things simultaneously, hence priorities have to be assigned to the performance objectives.

4   There are three main types of policy decision.
Design decisions are those which relate to the number, size, location of plants, product/service design, layout technology and human resources.

Planning and control decisions are those concerned with capacity adjustments and the systems which manage the delivery of products and services.

Improvement decisions are those focused on monitoring and improving the operation's performance.

5   Limited resources are one problem, but there are others.
There are usually a variety of ways in which performance of a firm can be improved. To improve product quality, for example, one could invest in advanced manufacturing technology, and/or simplify the assembly process, and/or employ more inspectors, and/or increase the use of statistical process control, and/or introduce a supplier ranking programme, and/or implement total quality management, etc. One problem is that companies do not have the resources to do all of the things they might wish to.

A second problem is that even if they did, some of the programmes, e.g. employ more inspectors and implement total quality management, might conflict with one another.

An organization needs a logical and holistic decision process which helps it determine what it should seek to do at a particular point in time, and why.

Formulating an operations strategy is one way of doing this.

The nature and content of operations strategy

The content of operations strategy

The process of operations strategy

A statement of the principles and policies which guide the operation's activities

The way in which the guiding principles and policies are developed

Prioritised performance objectives for each product/service group

Strategies for each decision area

Design

Planning and control

Improvement

OHP13

The relative importance of the performance objectives

Points to make

1 There are three main influences on the relative importance.
The relative importance of the performance objectives is a function of: (a) the specific needs of the company's customer groups; (b) the activities of the company's competitors; and (c) the stage the product/service is in its life cycle.

2 Different customers want different things.
If your customers purchase your products/services because you offer low prices, then low cost becomes important. If your customers want error-free products/services, then quality becomes important. If they want fast delivery, then speed becomes important. If they want reliable delivery, then dependability becomes important. If they want a wide range of products/services, or innovative ones, then flexibility becomes important.

3 Most companies have to satisfy various groups of customers.
Rarely does a company have a single homogeneous set of customers. Take, for example, an airline which serves both business passengers and holidaymakers. One set of customers, the business passengers, wants to arrive at its destination fresh and ready to work. Quality of service, rather than cost, is often its primary concern. Many holidaymakers, on the other hand, are less likely to care sufficiently about quality of service to pay extra for it - i.e. cost is more important than quality of service for them. The fact that different groups of customers have different requirements means that organizations sometimes need to set up independent operating systems - e.g. the division between economy and business class passengers.

4 Customer preferences change.
Different groups of customers are not the only problem, for customer preferences change over time. More and more businesses, for example, are now asking their staff to fly economy rather than business class because 'industry' has decided it cannot afford the extra cost incurred.

5 The competition also influences customer preferences.
Competitor actions can influence what customers value. Take, for example, the computer industry where Apple's 'what you see is what you get' policy has had major ramifications. Traditionally computer users accepted that they had to enter long strings of apparently meaningless characters to access their system. Now 'user-friendliness' is a major selling feature.

6 Order-winning and order-qualifying criteria.
A useful way of assessing the relative importance of the performance objectives is to decide whether a given performance objective is an order-winning or an order-qualifying criterion. Order-winning criteria are those things which directly and significantly contribute to winning business. They are regarded by customers as key reasons for purchasing the product or service. They are, therefore, the most important aspects of the way a company defines its competitive stance. Raising performance in an order-winning factor will either result in more business or improve the chances of gaining more business.

Order-qualifying criteria may not be the major competitive determinants of success, but are important in another way. They are those aspects of competitiveness where the operation's performance has to be above a particular level even to be considered by the customer. Below this 'qualifying' level of performance the company probably won't even be considered by many customers. Above the 'qualifying level', it will be considered, but mainly in terms of its performance in the order-winning criteria. Any further improvement in qualifying factors above the qualifying level is unlikely to gain much competitive benefit.

Relative importance of performance objectives

The influence of the organization's competitors

The relative importance of each performance objective to the operation

The influence of the organization's customers

The stage of the organization's products and services in its life cycle

The impact of the product life cycle

Points to make

1   There are four stages in a product's life cycle.

During the course of its 'life' a product/service passes through four main stages:

- introduction - when the product/service is first introduced. This stage is characterized by slow growth in sales.

- growth - when the product/service gains market acceptance. This stage is characterized by rapid growth in sales volume.

- maturity - when the market needs start to be fulfilled. This stage is characterized by sales slow down and level off.

- decline - when the market needs have been largely met. This stage is characterized by sales decline.

2   The importance of the performance objectives varies.

During each stage of the product life cycle the relative importance of the performance objectives varies.

Introduction. When a product/service is first introduced it is likely to be presented to the market on the basis that it is offering something new in terms of design or performance. If the product/service is really novel few if any competitors will be offering the same product/service and, because the number of customers is relatively low and because their needs are possibly not perfectly understood, the design of the product/service could be subject to frequent change. Given the relatively high uncertainty inherent in these market conditions the operations management of the company can best contribute by developing the flexibility to cope with changes in the specification of the product/service and possibly also in output volume. At the same time they will also need to maintain quality levels so as not to undermine the performance of the product/service which is the main basis of competition.

Growth. If the product/service survives the rigours of its introduction to the market it will begin to be more widely adopted. Increasing numbers of customers will accept the value of the product/service and volume will start to grow - perhaps rapidly. Competitors, seeing the attractiveness of the product/service, start to develop their own versions both to keep up with the market and to protect their own position within it. Within the growing market different customer groups will probably start to emerge and the design of the product/ service could start to standardize. Standardization is actually quite helpful in that it allows the operation to supply the rapidly growing market. In fact keeping up with demand could prove to be the main preoccupation of operations. Rapid and dependable response to demand will help to keep demand buoyant while ensuring that the company keeps its share of the market as competition starts to increase. The increasing competition also means that the company cannot afford to let its quality levels drop as it ramps up its level of activity.

Maturity. After their period of rapid growth, products and services are no longer the novel or even the 'up-and-coming' forces in the market. Demand begins to level off and hence the basis of competition for the remaining customers shifts to price and dependable supply.

Decline. When the product/service has been in the market for some time and demand has largely been met the basis of competition shifts almost entirely to price.

The impact of the product life cycle

Stage	Introduction	Growth	Maturity	Decline
Volume	Low	Rapid growth	High and level	Declining
Customers	Innovators	Early adopters	Bulk of market	Laggards
Competitors	Few/none	Increasing number	Stable number	Declining number
Variety of product or service	High customization	Increasingly standardised	Emerging dominant types	Commodity standardization
Likely order winners	Performance or novelty	Availability of quality products and services	Low price, dependable supply	Low price
Likely order qualifiers	Quality, product range	Price, product range	Product range, quality	Dependable supply
Operations performance objectives	Flexibility Quality	Speed Dependability Quality	Cost Dependability	Cost

The operations strategy decision areas and their impact

Points to make

1 There are two major categories of decision areas.

The main strategic decisions within operations management fall into two categories - structural and infrastructural. The chapter headings in this book (a) design decisions; (b) planning and control decisions; and (c) improvement decisions map on to these categories.

2 Structural decisions are concerned with ...

- New product/service development strategy - should the operation develop its own products? If so, how?

- Vertical integration strategy - should the operation expand by acquiring its suppliers or customers? If so, who should it acquire and why?

- Facilities strategy - what number of geographically separate sites should the operation have? Where should they be? What should they do?

- Technology strategy - what broad types of technology should the operation be using? What types of technology, if any, should it be developing?

3 Infrastructural decisions are concerned with ...

- Workforce and organization strategy - what role should the people who staff the operation play in its management? How should responsibilities for the activities of the operations function be split between the different groups?

- Capacity adjustment strategy - how should the operation forecast and monitor demand?

- Supplier development strategy - how should the operation choose its suppliers? How should it develop its relationship with its suppliers?

- Inventory strategy - how much inventory should the operation have? Where should it be located?

- Planning and control systems strategy - what systems should the operation use to plan its future activities?

- Improvement process strategy - who should be involved in the improvement process? What should they do? How fast should the operation expect/seek to improve?

- Performance measurement strategy - how should the performance of the operation be measured? How should the operation decide whether its performance is satisfactory?

- Failure prevention and recovery strategy - how should the operation maintain its resources so as to prevent failure? How should the operation plan to cope with a failure if one occurs?

4 The impact of these decisions.

To an extent every decision made will have an impact on every performance objective. Some strategies, however, will be particularly influential on certain objectives. The actual impact will depend to some extent on the organization being considered.

Operations strategy decision areas and their impact

	Q	S	D	F	C
New product/service development	√				√
Vertical integration strategy		√	√		√
Facilities strategy		√	√	√	√
Technology strategy	√			√	√
Workforce and organization strategy	√			√	√
Capacity adjustment strategy	√	√	√	√	√
Supplier development strategy	√	√	√		√
Inventory strategy		√	√		√
Planning and control systems	√	√	√		√
Improvement process strategy	√	√	√	√	√
Failure prevention and recovery	√		√		√

How operations strategies are put together

Points to make

1 How are operations strategies developed?

Operations managers can either adopt generic strategies, common approaches to organizing the operations function, or develop company-specific strategies.

Two well established processes for helping managers develop company-specific strategies are the Hill methodology and the Platts-Gregory methodology.

2 Strategy formulation methodologies have common elements.

Most strategy formulation methodologies: (a) provide a process which formally links the organization's strategic objectives to resource level objectives; (b) use competitive factors as the translation device between business strategy and operations strategy; (c) include a step which involves judging the relative importance of the various competitive factors in terms of customers' preference; (d) include a step which involves assessing current achieved performance, usually as compared against competitor performance levels; (e) emphasize that operations strategy formulation is an iterative process; and (f) build on the concept of 'ideal' or 'green field' models - if you were starting from scratch what would you do.

3 The effectiveness of an operations strategy can be assessed.

Operation strategies should be: (a) appropriate - they should show the operations function how it can best support the company's competitive strategy; (b) comprehensive - they should indicate how all parts of the operation are expected to perform; (c) coherent - the policies recommended for each part of the function should all point roughly in the same direction; (d) consistent over time - the lead time of operations improvement means that consistency must be maintained over a reasonable time period; and (e) credible - the strategy must be regarded as achievable otherwise it will not be supported.

How operations strategies are put together

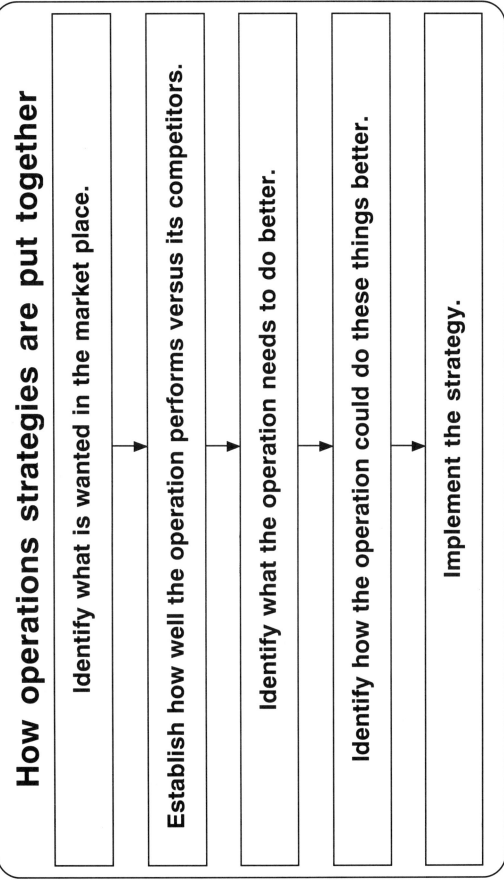

Identify what is wanted in the market place.

→

Establish how well the operation performs versus its competitors.

→

Identify what the operation needs to do better.

→

Identify how the operation could do these things better.

→

Implement the strategy.

OHP17

CHAPTER 4

DESIGN IN OPERATIONS MANAGEMENT

Key questions
• What is design in operations management?
• What objectives should the design activity have?
• How can design decisions be made?
• How does the design activity differ in different types of operation?
• What are 'process types'?

Topics covered
• The nature and purpose of the design activity in operations.
• The way in which the purpose of the design activity must always be to satisfy customers.
• The way which products, services and processes are designed.
• The way in which the range of design options narrows during the design activity.
• How design can be considered to be a decision-making process.
• Process types in manufacture and service.

Summary

What is design in operations management?
• Design is the activity which shapes the physical form and purpose of both products and services and the processes which produce them. It is an activity which starts with a concept and ends in the translation of that concept into a specification of something which can be created.
• The overall purpose of the design activity is to meet the needs of customers whether through the design of the products or services themselves, or through the design of the processes which will produce them.

What objectives should the design activity have?
• The design activity can be viewed as a transformation process in the same way as any other operation. It therefore can be judged in terms of its quality, speed, dependability, flexibility and cost.
• These objectives are more likely to be satisfied if the complementary activities of product or service design and process design are co-ordinated in some way.
• The design activity must also take account of environmental issues. These include examination of the source and suitability of materials, the sources and quantities of energy consumed, the amount and type of waste material, the life of the product itself and the end-of-life state of the product.

How can design decisions be made?
• Design is a multi-stage process which moves from concept through to a detailed specification.
• At each stage it is important to understand the design option and evaluate these in terms of their feasibility, acceptability and vulnerability.
• As the design activity progresses through its stages uncertainty regarding the finished design is reduced. This makes it increasingly difficult to change previous decisions.

How does the design activity differ in different types of operation?
• The key characteristics of an operation which determines the nature of its design activity are the volume and variety of its output.
• An operation's position on the volume-variety continuum influences many aspects of its design activity, including the emphasis which is placed on either product/service design or process design, the location policy it chooses, the standardization of its products and services, its choice of process technology, the nature of its layout and flow, the staff skills which it will require.

What are 'process types'?
• Process types are general approaches to managing the transformation process and depend on the volume and variety of an operations output.
• In manufacturing, these process types are (in order of increasing volume and decreasing variety) project, jobbing, batch, mass and continuous processes
• In service operations, although there is less consensus on the terminology, the terms often used (again in order of increasing volume and decreasing variety) are professional services, service shops, and mass services.

The nature and purpose of the design activity

Points to make

1 All operations managers are designers.

All operations managers make decisions which shape the design of the manufacturing or service delivery process - e.g. buying new equipment, changing the layout of the operation. These decisions often have implications for the products and services offered.

Operations managers also have an influence on the technical design of the products and services. Operations managers have to provide designers with information which specifies what the operation can do.

2 Key issues concerning design.

The purpose of design is to satisfy customer needs.

Products, services, and the processes which make products and deliver services all have to be designed.

The design activity is a transformation process.

The design process involves translating a concept into a specification.

3 The four Cs of design.

- Creativity - design requires the creation of something that has not existed before.

- Complexity - design involves decisions on a large number of parameters and variables.

- Compromise - design requires balancing multiple and sometimes conflicting requirements.

- Choice - design requires making choices between many options.

4 Increasing environmental awareness means design will change.

Key issues include:

- source of materials used in a product;

- quantities and sources of energy consumed in a process;

- the amount and type of waste material that is created during the manufacturing process;

- the life of the product itself;

- the end-of-life of the product - can the product be disposed of safely? Can it be recycled?

A major problem designers face is that these factors tradeoff with one another.

5 Lifecycle analysis is being used to explore these tradeoffs.

Lifecycle analysis involves assessing the energy costs of producing, running and disposing of a product.

Nature and purpose of the design activity

- Products, services and the processes which produce them all have to be designed.

- Decisions taken during the design of a product or service will have an impact on the decisions taken during the design of the process which produces those products or services and vice versa.

The purpose of design is to satisfy customers

Points to make

1   **The purpose of the design activity is to satisfy both internal and external customers.**

2   **Different types of designers have different perspectives.**
Product and service designers seek to create things which:

- are aesthetically pleasing;

- satisfy needs;

- meet expectations;

- perform well;

- are reliable;

- are easy to manufacture and deliver.

Operations managers tend to focus on the design of the transformation process. The wrong technology or a jumbled layout will limit the ability of the organization to meet its customers' needs.

3   **Poor product, service or process design will negatively impact the organization's ability to achieve its performance objectives.**

The purpose of design is to satisfy customers

- Product designers will seek to create things that:

  - are aesthetically pleasing;

  - satisfy needs;

  - meet expectations;

  - perform well;

  - are reliable;

  - are easy to manufacture and deliver.

- Operations managers tend to focus on the design of the transformation process.

Products, services and processes are all designed

Points to make

1 Product/service and process design are interrelated.
It is pointless committing to a detailed product design without considering how the product can be made.

Changing product or service designs can have major process implications, especially in terms of cost.

Existing processes provide design constraints.

2 Product/service and process design have to be managed together.
Product/service designs should be evaluated in terms of their implications for processing costs as well as their functionality.

3 Achieving the speed objective.
Reducing time to market involves managing the product/service and process overlap carefully.

Often this overlap is greater in services, as services can rarely be separated from the process which delivers them.

Product, service and process design

Products/services should be designed so that they can be created effectively

Processes should be designed so that they can create all products/services the operation may introduce

Design of the product

Design of the process

Decisions taken during the design of the product/service impact upon the process which produces it and vice versa

OHP20

The range of design options narrows during the activity

Points to make

1 The design activity is a transformation process.

Inputs to the design activity include:

- Transformed resources - information in the form of market forecasts, market preferences and technical data.

- Transforming resources - administrative, technical and clerical staff, computer-aided design systems, development and testing equipment.

The actual design process is concerned with changing the informational properties of the inputs, and sometimes with changing physical properties (e.g. producing prototypes).

2 The objectives of the design activity can be considered in terms of the five performance objectives.

All operations satisfy their customers by producing their services and goods according to the customers' desires for quality, speed, dependability, flexibility and cost. The design activity is no exception.

3 The design activity involves progressively reducing uncertainty.

The design process can be split into stages. At each stage, as options are eliminated, uncertainty surrounding the design decreases.

An implication of this is that it becomes more expensive to change a design the closer the design process is to completion.

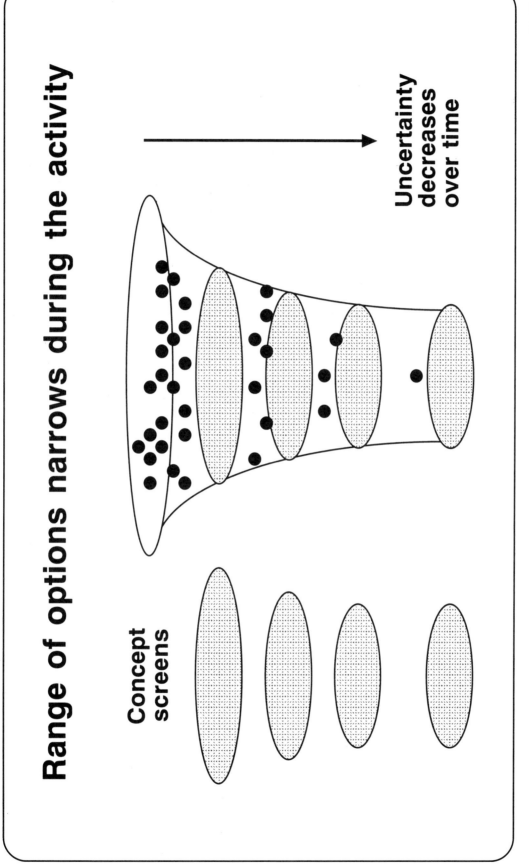

Range of options narrows during the activity

Concept screens

Uncertainty decreases over time

OHP21

The design activity is a decision-making process

Points to make

1 The design activity involves identifying and evaluating options.
Designers have continually to identify and evaluate how the objectives of the design can be achieved.

In the early stages of the design activity the options that have to be considered will be far broader than those that have to be considered in the later stages.

2 If options are to be evaluated design criteria are necessary.

3 There are three basic design criteria.
Feasibility - can we do it (the investment)?:
- Do we have the skills (quality of resources) to cope with this option?
- Do we have the organizational capacity (quantity of resources) to cope with this option?
- Do we have the financial resources to cope with this option?

Acceptability - do we want to do it (the return)?:
- Does this option satisfy the performance criteria which the design is trying to achieve?
- Will this option give a satisfactory financial return?

Vulnerability - do we want to take the risk (the risk)?:
- Do we understand the full consequences of adopting this option?
- Being pessimistic, what could go wrong if we adopt the option and what would be the consequences if everything went wrong?

4 Simulation has a major role to play in the design activity.
As design involves the designer making decisions before the product or service has been created, the designer cannot be sure of the consequences of their decisions.

Simulation, used in a predictive mode, is one way of increasing the probability that the designer will make the right decision.

Simulations can vary from physical to computer models. An interesting, and relatively recent development, is virtual reality.

Design activity is a decision-making process

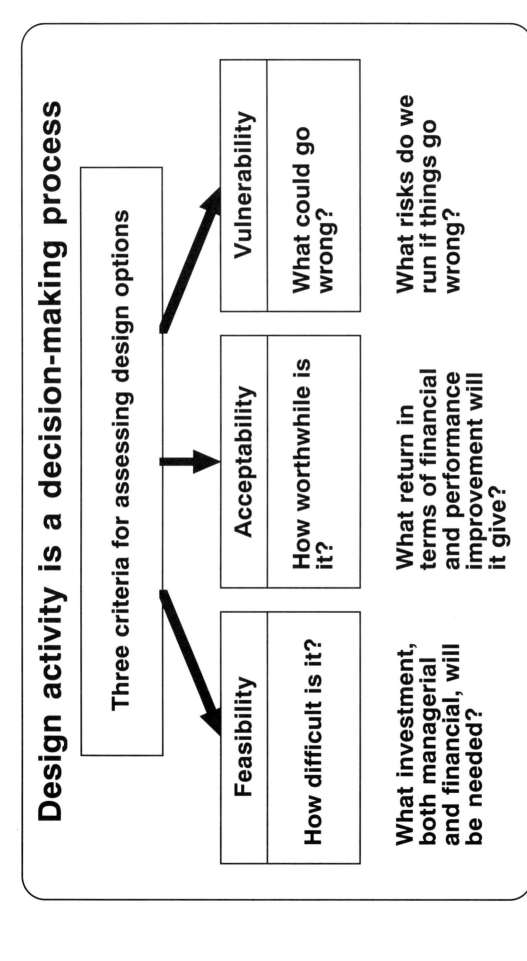

Three criteria for assessing design options

Feasibility

How difficult is it?

What investment, both managerial and financial, will be needed?

Acceptability

How worthwhile is it?

What return in terms of financial and performance improvement will it give?

Vulnerability

What could go wrong?

What risks do we run if things go wrong?

Process types in manufacture and service

Points to make

1 Process and service design are influenced by volume and variety.

Once an organization has chosen where to position itself on the volume/variety matrix it has decided what some of its performance objectives will be and limited further product, service and process design.

2 The impact of volume and variety on the performance objectives.

Quality - if volumes are low the operation will seek to customize products/services. Speed - if volumes are low the operation will seek to negotiate delivery times on an item-by-item basis. Dependability - if volumes are low the operation will seek to meet individually negotiated delivery promises. Flexibility - if volumes are low the operation will seek product flexibility. Cost - if volumes are low the operation is likely to have a high unit cost. If volumes are high the operation is likely to have a low unit cost.

3 The impact of volume and variety on the design activity.

Operations with low volumes and high variety will: (a) have little design standardization; (b) invest in general technology; (c) have to cope with complex flows of information; and (d) have to employ highly skilled people.

Operations with high volumes and low variety will: (a) have little design variety; (b) invest in dedicated equipment; and (c) need system management skills.

4 The impact of volume and variety on process design.

There are five basic process designs. In order of appropriateness for increasing volume and decreasing variety these are: (a) project - each project has its own start and finish times. Resources are dedicated to particular projects for their duration; (b) jobbing - each product shares resources with many other different products; (c) batch - products are produced in batches of varying sizes. Each part of the operation has periods when it is repeating an activity; (d) mass - high volume and essentially repetitive. Low variety in terms of the basic product; and (e) continuous - very high volumes and predictable flow. Usually capital intensive and inflexible.

5 The impact of volume and variety on process design for services.

There are three basic process designs for services. In order of appropriateness for increasing volume and decreasing variety these are: (a) professional services - high-contact operations which tend to be people based (e.g. consulting company); (b) service shops - mixture of front- and back-office activities, (e.g. a bank); and (c) mass services - many customer transactions, limited contact time and little customization, (e.g. supermarkets).

6 The product-process matrix can be used to describe the implications of volume and variety.

The product-process matrix represents process choice on a matrix with volume-variety as one dimension and process types as another. The diagonal describes the lowest cost position for a given type of operation.

Operations to the right of the diagonal could save money by further standardization of their processes. Operations to the left of the diagonal could save money by enhancing their flexibility.

Process types in manufacturing

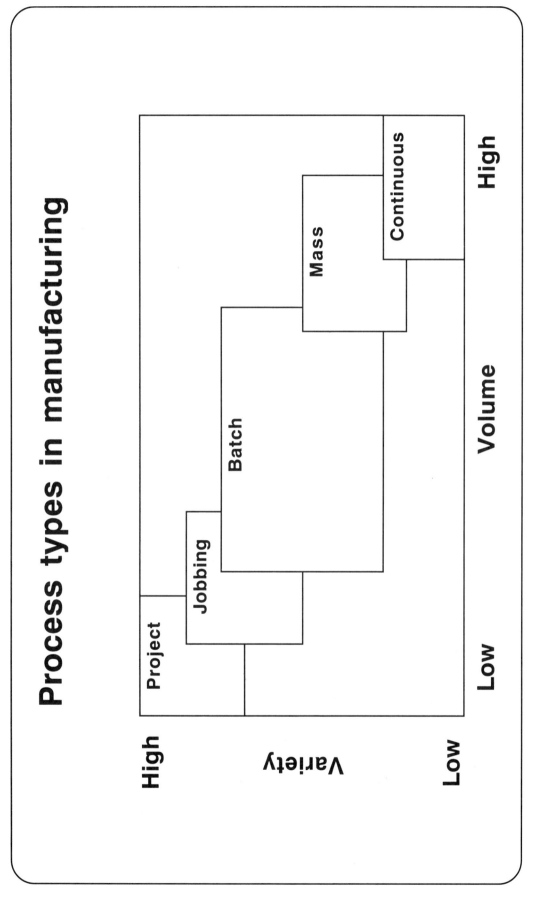

OHP23

CHAPTER 5

THE DESIGN OF PRODUCTS AND SERVICES

Key questions
• Why is good product and service design important?
• What are the stages in product and service design?
• Why should product and service design and process design be considered interactively?
• How should interactive design be managed?

Topics covered
• The aspects of products and services which need designing. More specifically, how design affects the concept, the package, and the process which comprise the product or service.
• The outputs from the product and service design activity.
• The stages which are involved in designing any product or service.
The recent 'interactive' approaches to concurrent and multi-disciplinary design which encourage fast and efficient time-to-market.

Summary:
Why is good product and service design important?
• Good product and service design translates customer needs into the shape and form of the product or service and by doing this specifies the required capabilities of the operation. Therefore product and service design in effect connects the operation itself to its customers.
• This translation process includes formalizing three particularly important issues for operations managers. These are the concept, package, and process implied by the design.
• Companies like Braun have found that good aesthetic and functional design enhances their profitability.

What are the stages in product and service design?
• 'Concept generation' transforms an idea for a product or service into a concept which indicates the form, function, purpose and benefits of the idea.
• 'Screening' the concept involves examining its acceptability in broad terms to ensure that it is a sensible addition to the company's product or service portfolio. Market, financial and operations evaluation must all be carried out during the screening process.
• 'Preliminary design' involves the identification of all the component parts of the product or service and the way they fit together. Typical tools used during this phase include activity/product structures, bills of materials and flow charts.
• 'Design evaluation and improvement' involves re-examining the design to see if it can be done in a better way, more cheaply or more easily. Typical techniques used here include quality function deployment, value engineering and Taguchi methods.
• 'Prototyping and final design' involves providing the final details which allow the product or service to be produced. Computer aided design (CAD) is often used at this point, although it may also be used elsewhere in the design process. The outcome of this stage is a fully developed specification for the package of products and services as well as a specification for the processes that will make and deliver them to customers.

• Why should product and service design and process design be considered interactively?

• Looking at them together can improve the quality of both product and service design and process design. Considering the constraints of the operation during product and service design ensures that the final designs are 'producable'. Considering product and service design during process design ensures that processes are developed with the long-term needs of products and services in mind.

• Interactive design helps fast time to market. This ensures that the company will break even on its investment in the new design earlier than would otherwise have been the case.

How should interactive design be managed?

• Employing 'simultaneous development' where design decisions are taken as early as they can be, without necessarily waiting for a whole design phase to be completed. Such early commitment of design resources must also include effective communication between the phases in design activity.

• Ensuring early 'conflict resolution' which allows contentious decisions to be resolved early in the design process, thereby not allowing them to cause far more delay and confusion if they emerge later on.

• Using 'project-based organization structure' which can ensure that a focused and coherent team of designers are dedicated to a single design or group of design projects.

Aspects of products and services which need designing

Points to make

1 The objective of product or service is to satisfy customers.
Various functions have a role to play.

Marketing has to gather information so that the needs and wants of the customers can be understood.

Product and service designers have to create specifications which define products or services which will satisfy these needs and wants.

Operations has to take these specifications and use them to produce the product or service.

2 There are three aspects of a product or service that need designing.
The concept - this is not a physical statement of bits, rather it should summarize the way the customer and the organization perceive the benefits of the product or service.

The package - most things we buy consist of both products and services. The package should explain these component products and services, which together provide the benefits described in the concept.

A distinction can be made between those elements of the package which are core and those which are supporting. Core products and services are those that cannot be removed from the package without destroying the nature of the package. Supporting products and services enhance the package, but are not core to it.

The process - how the product or service will actually be produced. Given that most products and services consist of sub-products and services, various processes are likely to be required.

Aspects of product and service design

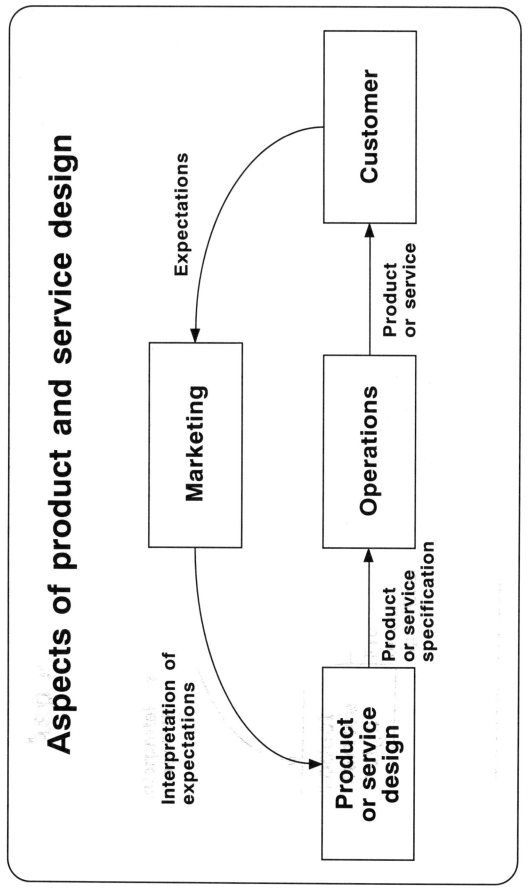

The outputs from the product or service design activity

Points to make

1   The final outcome of the product or service design activity is a fully detailed specification of the product or service.

2   The concept specifies the form, function and overall purpose of the design.
    The concept should also specify the benefits the design will provide.

3   The package specifies the collection of individual products and services required to provide and support the concept.

4   The process specifies how the various individual products and services in the package are to be produced.

5   The design activity consists of a series of stages:
    • Concept generation.

    • Concept screening.

    • Preliminary design.

    • Evaluation and improvement.

    • Prototyping and final design.

The outputs from product and service design

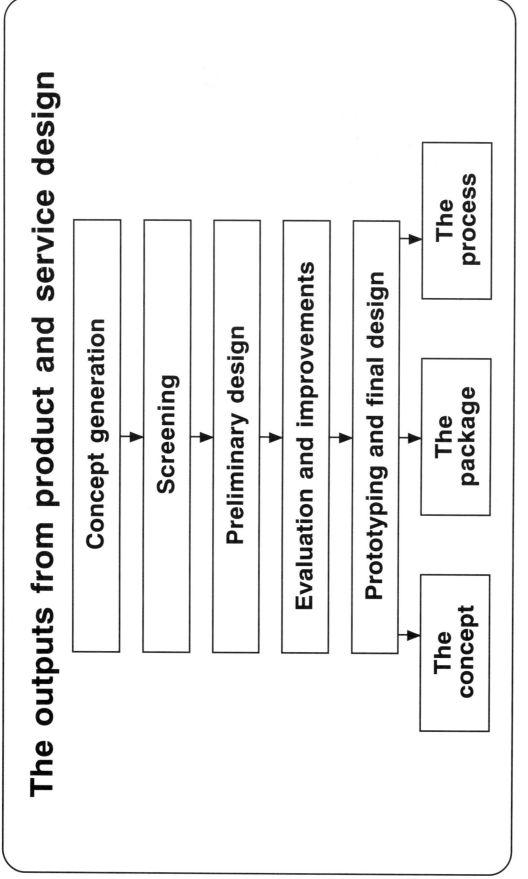

Concept generation → Screening → Preliminary design → Evaluation and improvements → Prototyping and final design → The concept, The package, The process

Product and service concept generation

Points to make

1 Ideas and concepts are not synonymous.
Concepts are operationalized ideas. Concepts are ideas with form, function and purpose.

2 Ideas come from various sources.
Ideas can arise from sources both within and outside the organization.

3 Ideas can come from customers.
Marketing is responsible for identifying potential opportunities. Sources of data include focus groups and simply 'listening to the customer'.

Focus groups:

• Groups of seven to ten people.

• Ideally the people in the group should not know each other, but should know something about the issue being discussed.

• A concept researcher should be used to stimulate discussion.

• The process should be repeated several times with different groups so that common themes can be drawn out.

Listening to the customer:

• Review customer complaints.

• Train sales staff to probe for information during the sales process.

• A key issue is how the information generated is captured.

4 Ideas can come from competitors.
A useful technique is reverse engineering. This involves stripping down competitors' products. In addition to stimulating new ideas, reverse engineering can provide information on novel designs.

5 Ideas can come from staff.
Although many of the ideas for new products or services will come from members of the research and development department, it is important to recognize that other members of the organization can contribute. Once again a key issue is how such ideas can be captured.

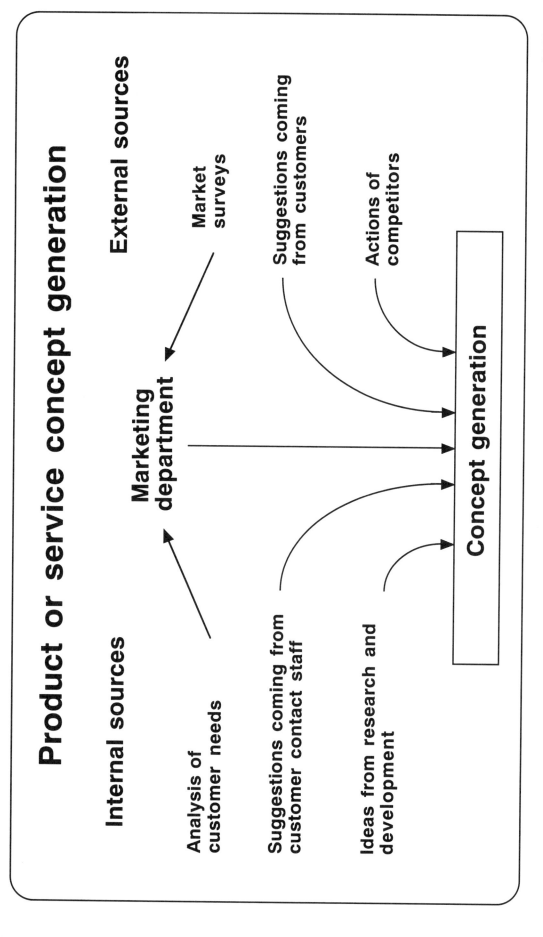

Product or service concept generation

Internal sources

Analysis of customer needs

Suggestions coming from customer contact staff

Ideas from research and development

External sources

Market surveys

Suggestions coming from customers

Actions of competitors

Marketing department

Concept generation

OHP26

Screening of the concept

Points to make

1   Not all concepts can be converted into designs.
Designers have to be selective. The purpose of screening is to take concepts and evaluate their feasibility, acceptability and vulnerability.

2   Concepts often have to pass through several screens.
Different functions, each of which will have different criteria, can be involved in the screening process.

3   Key questions for marketing will include:
Will the concept work in the market?

Is the concept too similar to, or too different from, competing products or services?

Will there be sufficient demand for the product or service to make it worthwhile?

Will the concept fit within the framework provided by the existing marketing policy?

4   Key questions for operations will include:
Will we be able to produce this product or provide this service?

Do we have the capacity?

Do we have the human resources?

Do we have the technology?

How much will it cost to produce this product or provide this service?

5   Key questions for finance will include:
Given the volumes being predicted by marketing, and the costs being predicted by operations:

What are the financial implications of this product or service?

What capital investment will we have to make?

What will our operating costs be?

What will our profit margins be?

What will the pay-back rate be?

Screening the concepts

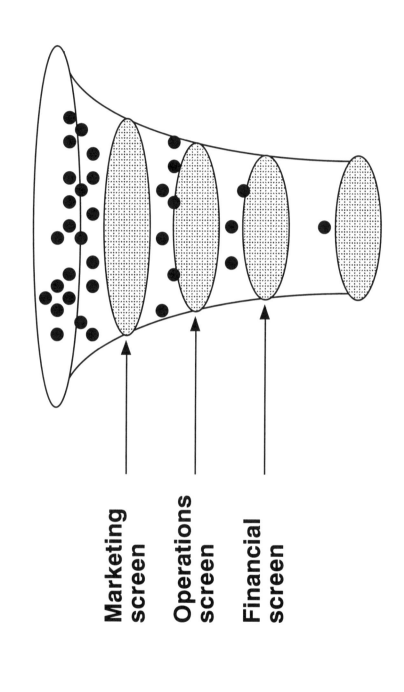

Marketing
screen

Operations
screen

Financial
screen

Preliminary design of the product or service

Points to make

1 Preliminary design involves having a 'first stab' at:
- specifying the component products and services in the package;

- identifying which processes will be used to create the component elements which together make up the package.

2 Specifying the components of the package involves defining what will go into the package.
To do this information has to be collected on:
- the component parts;

- the product or service structure - the order in which the component parts have to be put together;

- the bill of materials (BOM) - the quantity of each component or part in the final package.

3 There are many techniques for documenting (blueprinting) which processes should be used.
All of these techniques have two features. First, they identify the different activities that take place during processing. Second, they show how materials and/or people flow through the operation.

Four of the more common techniques are:

Simple flow charts:
- Can be used to identify the main elements in a process.
- Also show how materials and information flow through the process.

Routing sheets (operations process charts):
- Provide information about the activities involved in the process.
- Describe which tools are needed and the activities involved.

Process flow charts:
- Use symbols to identify different types of activity.
- Permit more detailed design and evaluation of design.

Customer processing framework:
- Devised specifically for customer flows.
- Identifies key activities that occur when customers are being processed. These include:

  - Selection - the customer choosing which operation to use.
  - Point of entry - the point at which the customer enters the service process.
  - Response time - how long the customer has to wait before being processed.
  - Point of impact - the moment the service worker starts to deal with the customer.
  - Delivery - the part of the process which actually delivers the core service.
  - Point of departure - the point at which the customer leaves the service process.
  - Follow up - the activities of the service staff after processing to check up on the customer.

Preliminary design of the product or service

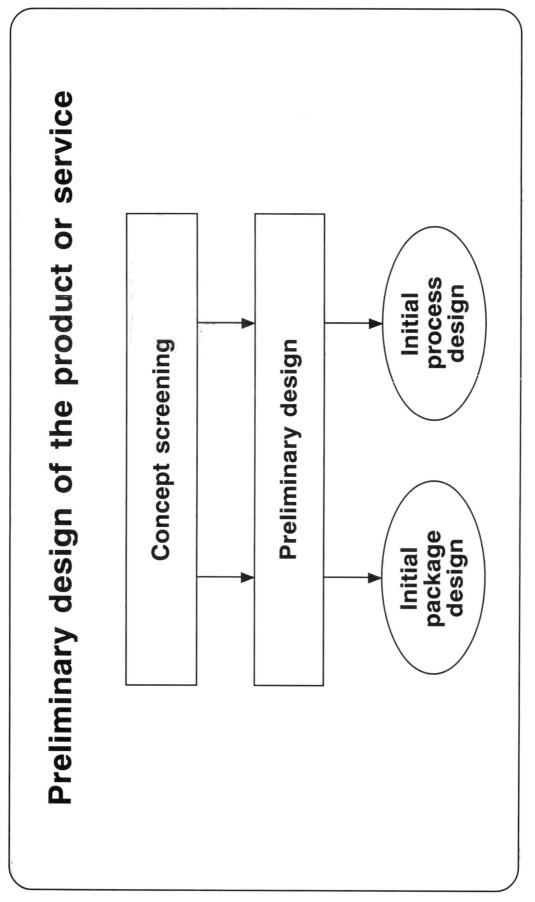

OHP28

Evaluating and improving the preliminary design

Points to make

1   Once the preliminary design has been produced it should be evaluated to see if it can be improved.
This should take place prior to market testing.

2   There are various ways in which the preliminary design can be evaluated.
These include quality function deployment (QFD), value engineering, and Taguchi methods.

3   Quality function deployment aims to ensure that the final design actually satisfies the customer's needs.
Quality function deployment, also known as the 'house of quality' because of its shape, was developed at Mitsubishi's Kobe shipyard. QFD seeks to capture what the customer needs and to identify how these needs might be satisfied.

Customer needs may not have been explicitly considered since the concept generation phase. Hence, when evaluating the preliminary design, it is appropriate to check whether the proposed design is likely to satisfy them.

4   Value engineering aims to prevent unnecessary cost being designed into a product or service.
Value engineering seeks to eliminate any costs that do not contribute to the value and performance of the product or service.

It does this by:
* identifying which parts of the product or service are core (primary) and which are supporting (secondary);

* determining how much each part of the product or service costs;

* establishing whether any parts of the product or service have disproportionate costs (e.g. secondary components that are very expensive);

* re-designing these.

Value engineering projects are usually conducted by multi-disciplinary teams consisting of operations personnel, financial analysts, designers and purchasing specialists. Value engineering requires innovative and critical thinking.

Costs are reduced by reducing the number of components, using cheaper materials and simplifying the processes involved.

5   Taguchi methods seek to test the robustness of designs.
The basic premise underlying the Taguchi methodology is that products and services should perform even in hostile environments. The methodology consists of three things:
* The Taguchi loss function - shows the target should always be the nominal tolerance.

* Orthogonal arrays - used to simplify experimental design.

* Visual analysis - used to analyse data.

Evaluating and improving the preliminary design

- There are various ways of evaluating preliminary designs.

- These include:

  - quality function deployment;

  - value engineering;

  - Taguchi methods.

OHP29

Prototyping and final design

Points to make

1   The design has to be turned into a prototype so it can be tested.

2   Prototypes come in various forms including:
- card models;

- clay models;

- computer simulations.

3   In the service sector prototypes usually take the form of computer models.
Although sometimes services are implemented in a limited area on a pilot basis.

4   Computer-aided design (CAD), which can be used both as a drafting and a prototyping device, has proved to be extremely useful.
CAD has simplified the construction of prototypes either in the form of physical models or computer simulations.

In terms of hardware requirements CAD needs:

- an input device - joystick, light pen, mouse, electronic tablet, keyboard;

- a central processing unit and software;

- a means of storing data - disk, magnetic tape;

- a display;

- an output device - printer, plotter.

CAD software comes in various forms. The simplest packages can only be used for two dimensional modelling. More complex packages can be used for three dimensional modelling, either in wire-box, or full solid form. Two and a half dimensional (extruded two dimensional shapes) modelling packages also exist.

CAD has several advantages over conventional technology. These include CAD's ability to:

- store and retrieve design data rapidly;

- manipulate designs easily. CAD enhances flexibility as it simplifies the process of modifying old designs;

- hold libraries of standardized shapes. These reduce the possibilities of design error and also speed up the design process.

Prototyping and final design

- Prototypes are needed so products and services can be tested.

- Prototypes come in various forms:

  - card models;

  - clay models;

  - computer simulations.

- CAD has considerably simplified the production of prototypes.

Recent 'interactive' approaches

Points to make

1 Separating the design of the product or service from the design of the process is unwise.
Operations has inputs to make to the design activity from initial concept evaluation phase through to production and product launch.

The act of merging product and process design is known as interactive design.

2 Interactive design helps reduce time-to-market.
Reducing the time-to-market can:

- Provide a competitive advantage. The faster a business can introduce new products the easier it is for the business to take advantage of new and emerging technologies which may help improve the product's functionality.

- Reduce the organization's cost base. The longer the design process takes the greater the staff costs.

- Ease cash flows. During the design process the organization is investing money in a product, but receiving no income from it. The sooner the product is released the sooner the organization begins to get a return on its investment.

3 Time-to-market can be reduced by simultaneous development.
Traditionally design has been a sequential activity. Concept generation has taken place, before evaluation. Evaluation has taken place before preliminary design. The advantage of the sequential approach is that it is easy to manage, but it is time consuming and costly.

Simultaneous development involves starting the next phase once it can be started. Concepts can be evaluated once they have been generated. Preliminary designs can be drawn up once concepts have been approved.

The rational underlying simultaneous development, which is also known as concurrent engineering, is that if uncertainty reduces during each stage of the design activity, then there must be some point at which certainty is sufficiently high to begin the next stage, even though the preceding stage has not finished.

Effective communication between groups responsible for the various stages is vital if simultaneous development is to be successful.

4 Early conflict resolution is important.
Every decision that is made in the design activity commits money. Changing decisions costs money. The later decisions are changed the more it costs. Hence early conflict resolution is important.

5 Organizational structure also needs to be considered.
The design activity requires inputs from various functions. Team-based structures appear to be more effective than functional structures for this.

Interactive approaches to design

Sequential approach

| First stage in the design activity | Second stage in the design activity | Third stage in the design activity |

Simultaneous approach

| First stage in the design activity |
| Second stage in the design activity |
| Third stage in the design activity |

CHAPTER 6

DESIGN OF THE OPERATIONS NETWORK

Key questions
• Why should an organization take a total supply network perspective?
• How much of a network should an operation own?
• Where should an operation be located?
• How much capacity should an operation plan to have?

Topics covered
• The nature of operations networks and the concept of the 'supply-side' and the 'demand-side' parts of the network.
• The advantages of taking a network perspective in making strategic design decisions.
• The direction, extent and balance of the operation's vertical integration and how these factors can affect the performance of the operation.
• The location of operations, and how supply-side and demand-side influences determine location decisions.
• How the capacity of an operation is determined, and how long-term capacity levels are changed as demand changes over time.

Summary
Why should an organization take a total supply network perspective?
• The main advantage is that it helps any operation to understand how it can compete effectively within the network. This is because a supply network approach requires operations managers to think about their suppliers and their customers as *operations*.
• Taking a supply network perspective can also help to identify particularly significant links within the network and hence identify long-term strategic changes which will affect the operation.
• The starting point for all these advantages is taking a broad perspective not only of the immediate supply network (that is the customers and suppliers with which an operation has immediate contact) but also of the total supply network (that is all the significant operations on the supply side and the demand side of an operation).

How much of a network should an operation own?
• This issue is called the *vertical integration* decision and is defined by the direction of ownership, the extent of ownership and the type of relationships envisaged.
• The direction of ownership decision refers to whether an organization wants to own the operations on its supply-side (backwards integration) or on its demand-side (forward integration).
• The extent of ownership decision relates to how many of the demand-side or supply-side operations the organization wants to own.
• The nature of the relationship decision relates to whether stages in the network involve exclusive relationships in which each stage serves only its own in-house customers, or alternatively, where each stage is free to trade with parts of the network which are not owned by the organization.

Where should an operation be located?
• An existing operation will relocate only if the costs and disruption of moving are less than the benefits it believes it will gain from its new location.

• The stimuli which act on an organization during the location decision can be divided into supply-side and demand-side influences. Supply-side influences are the factors such as labour, land and utility costs which change as the location changes. Demand-side influences include such things as the image of the location, its convenience for customers, and the suitability of the site itself.

• All these factors can be applied (to different degrees) at three levels: the choice of a country or region, the choice of an area within a country or region, the choice of a specific site itself.

How much capacity should an operation plan to have?

• The amount of capacity an organization will have depends on its view of current and future demand. It is when its view of future demand is different from current demand that this issue becomes important.

• When an organization has to cope with changing demand a number of capacity decisions needs to be taken. These include choosing the optimum capacity for each site, balancing the various capacity levels of the operations in the network, and timing the changes in the capacity of each part of the network.

• Important influences on these decisions include the concepts of economy and diseconomy of scale, supply flexibility if demand is different from forecast and the profitability and cash-flow implications of capacity timing changes.

The nature of operations networks

Points to make

1 **Every operation is part of a network of suppliers and customers.**

Materials, parts, assemblies, information, ideas, people and money all flow through the network.

On the supply side all operations have suppliers who provide parts, information and services.

On the demand side all operations have customers, who may not be the end users of the product or service.

2 **The network can be described in terms of tiers.**

Direct suppliers and customers of a given operation are known as first-tier suppliers and customers. The suppliers to an operations first-tier suppliers are the operations second-tier suppliers, and so on.

3 **Usually operations deal only with their first-tier suppliers and customers, but this is not always the case.**

4 **An operation's immediate supply network consists of suppliers and customers who are in direct contact with the operation.**

An operations total supply network consists of all the suppliers and customers that the operations buys from or supplies to, no matter how indirectly.

5 **Networks involve two-way flow.**

Information, in the form of orders, flows from customers to suppliers and ripples down the chain.

Goods and materials flow from suppliers to customers.

The nature of the network

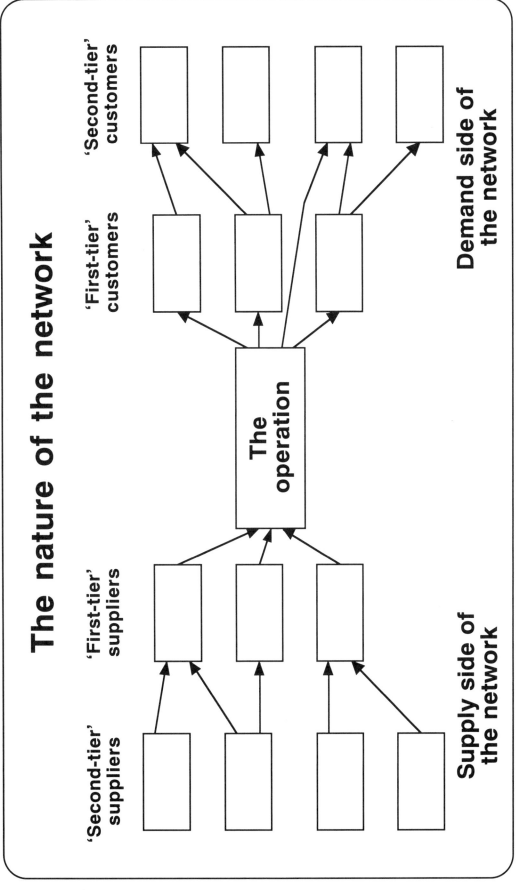

'Second-tier' suppliers

'First-tier' suppliers

The operation

'First-tier' customers

'Second-tier' customers

Supply side of the network

Demand side of the network

OHP32

Advantages of taking a network perspective

Points to make

1 Taking a network perspective helps a company understand how to compete effectively.

Operations need to look beyond their immediate customers to understand what the end users of their products and services want. There are two ways in which they can do this. Either they can rely on the opinions of others or they can find out for themselves.

2 Taking a network perspective helps identify particularly significant links in the network.

The key to understanding networks is to understand who contributes to achieving the performance objectives that are valued by the end customer. To analyse a network it is therefore necessary to:

- identify what the end customers want;

- identify who helps provide what the end customers want.

Not all parts of the network will be able to contribute equally to providing what the end customers want.

The best way for the network to win and retain end-customer business is for those parts of the network which cannot provide exactly what the end customer wants, to find out how they can support those parts which can.

3 Taking a network perspective helps a company focus on its long-term position in the network.

The balance of power in any network will vary over time. A key issue for a given operation is whether it should seek to exploit power when it has it. In the longer term this is probably not a sensible strategy. It might be better for the more powerful organizations to help the weaker organizations improve.

4 Taking a network perspective also highlights the three key network design decisions.
- Vertical integration.

- Operations location.

- Long-term capacity.

Advantages of taking a network perspective

Location of the operation
Where should the operation be located?

Taking a network perspective helps businesses address the three key network design decisions.

Vertical integration
How much of the network should the operation seek to own?

Balance of capacity
How should capacity be managed in the long-term?

Direction, extent and balance of vertical integration

Points to make

1   Vertical integration involves deciding how much of the network the operation should seek to own.

When making vertical integration decisions organizations have to assess how wise it is for them to buy their suppliers or customers.

At the product level vertical integration is all about the make-buy decision. It involves deciding what the operation should make and what it should buy in from outside.

2   Key issues associated with vertical integration are:

• Direction of expansion - whether to expand up or down the supply chain.

• Extent of process span - how far to expand.

• Balance of capacity - to what extent should capacity be balanced among the vertically integrated stages.

3   Direction of vertical integration.

Buying suppliers can provide cost advantages and makes competitors dependent on you. Such backward, or upstream, vertical integration is often considered a defensive move.

Buying customers brings the organization closer to the market.   Such forward, or downstream, vertical integration is often considered an offensive move.

4   Extent of vertical integration.

Once the organization has decided in which direction it wishes to expand, it has to decide how far it wishes to expand.

5   Balance of capacity.

The issue here is whether the organization should seek to balance capacity so that each stage in the chain only supplies the next stage, or whether it should let there be excess capacity which can be used to attack other markets.

The advantage of fully balanced networks is that they are simpler to manage and each business can focus on supplying its direct customers.

6   Benefits of vertical integration.

Being vertically integrated means that organizations are closer to their customers and suppliers. This makes it easier to trace and eliminate the root causes of any quality problems. In terms of speed, vertically integrated companies are better able to synchronize their schedules and, because of their closeness, find forecasting easier.   Better forecasts and improved communications lead to more accurate delivery promises and enhanced dependability. Technological advances, which can be denied to competitors, can be shared among the group giving better product flexibility.   The costs of research and development, and other support functions, can also be pooled. This reduces the group's cost base.

There is one major disadvantage of being vertically integrated which has to be set off against these advantages. Vertically integrated firms are not subject to market forces. Hence there is little stimulus for businesses to improve the level of service they provide.

Direction, extent and balance of vertical integration

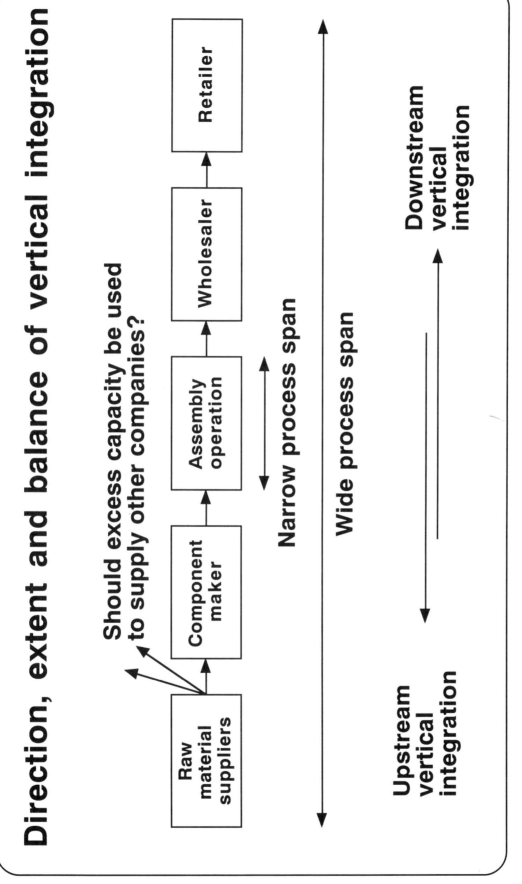

Should excess capacity be used to supply other companies?

| Raw material suppliers | → | Component maker | → | Assembly operation | → | Wholesaler | → | Retailer |

Narrow process span

Wide process span

Upstream vertical integration

Downstream vertical integration

The location of operations

Points to make

1 The location decision involves deciding where the operation should be located.

The location of an operation will have an effect on its cost base and the level of service it can provide. The actual impact will depend upon the operation's geographical position relative to its customers, suppliers and the resources it consumes.

2 Two reasons why operations need to make location decisions.

First, demand may increase or decrease and this may mean that new facilities have to be built, existing facilities have to be expanded, or existing facilities have to be closed. Second, the cost and/or availability of resources may change.

3 The objective of the location decision is to achieve a balance.

Different locations will have different implications for an operation in terms of: (a) spatially variable costs - costs that change depending on the location; (b) service - the level of service the operation is able to provide; and (c) revenue potential.

The objective of the location decision is to seek to balance these three items, ideally by minimizing spatial variable costs and maximizing service and revenue potential.

4 Various factors influence the location decision.

On the supply side the location decision is influenced by: (a) labour costs - wages and non-wage costs (employment taxes, holiday entitlements). These costs are not comparable from region to region. Factors such as productivity and exchange rates also have to be considered; (b) land costs; (c) energy costs; (d) transportation costs - both in terms of how much it will cost to ship products to the market and how much it will cost to bring resources to the operation; and (e) community factors - local tax rates, capital movement restrictions, government financial assistance, government planning assistance, political stability, local attitudes towards investment, language, local amenities (schools, theatres, shops), availability of support services, history of labour relations, labour absenteeism and turnover rates, environmental restrictions and waste disposal, planning procedures and restrictions.

On the demand side the location decision is influenced by: (a) labour skills; (b) convenience for customers; (c) the actual site; and (d) the image of the location.

5 The location decision has to consider various levels.

First, the location decision has to consider which region or country will be appropriate. Issues that need to be considered at this level include language and political stability. Second, the location decision has to consider which area within the region or country will be appropriate. Issues that need to be considered at this level include land prices, the local labour force, community factors and infrastructural development. Third, the location decision has to consider the actual site. Issues that need to be considered at this level include soil composition, future plans for the site, availability of utilities, shape of the site and ease of access. The choice of the actual site is often the most opportunistic decision that has to be made.

6 The location decision is largely based on judgment, although techniques which can be used do exist.

Two of the most common techniques are the weighted scoring method and the centre of gravity method.

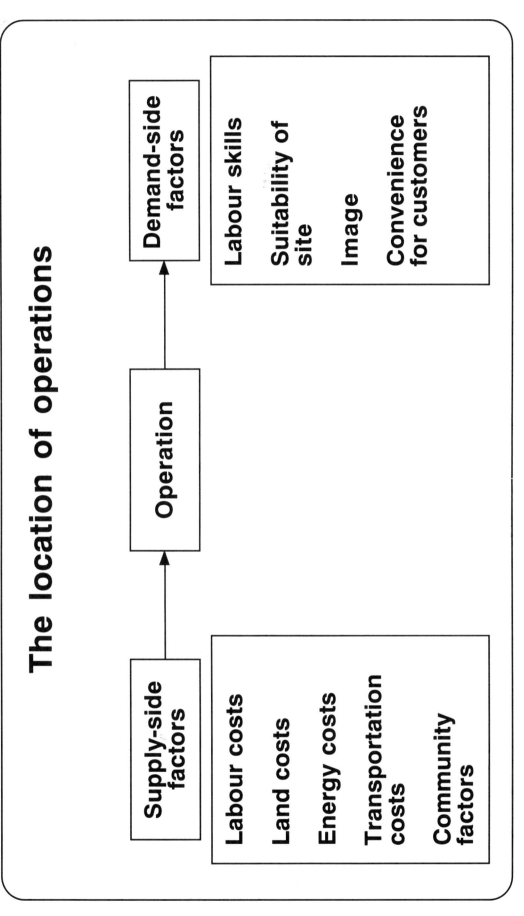

The location of operations

Demand-side factors

Labour skills

Suitability of site

Image

Convenience for customers

Operation

Supply-side factors

Labour costs

Land costs

Energy costs

Transportation costs

Community factors

The balance of capacity

Points to make

1   When designing operations networks an important consideration is long-term capacity management.

The basic question that we are trying to address here is what physical capacity should each part of the network have at a given point in time.

2   Production costs can be classified as fixed or variable.

Fixed costs exist irrespective of how much is produced. Variable costs increase as production volumes increase. Dividing the total output by the total fixed and variable cost gives the cost per unit.

3   Unit costs are lowest when all capacity is being used.

Although this is generally the case, there are some reasons why the statement that 'unit costs are at their lowest when all capacity is being used' is not entirely true.

- In most operations capacity is effectively infinite - work can be sub-contracted, overtime can be worked. Hence it is impossible to work at maximum capacity.

- Extra costs can be incurred when utilization is high. For example, machines may break down more frequently.

- All operations have 'fixed cost breaks' - points at which fixed costs come into play.

4   There are diseconomies of scale as well as economies of scale.

Economies of scale arise because fixed and capital costs are not proportional to plant size. Diseconomies of scale arise because transportation costs can be considerably higher for large plants and communication can be a major problem.

5   There are two basic strategies for capacity management - capacity leading demand and capacity lagging demand.

When capacity leads demand the operation should always have enough capacity to cope with demand, therefore revenue is maximized and customers are satisfied. The major problem with this strategy is that the utilization of the plant is usually low.

When capacity lags demand the operation will rarely have sufficient capacity to meet demand. Utilization will be high, but customers will remain unsatisfied.

6   One option is to smooth with inventory.

Spare capacity can be used to build inventory which can be used later. The major risk with this strategy is that the inventory may deteriorate or become obsolete.

7   Breakeven analysis is a useful means of calculating how much needs to be sold if the organization is to be profitable.

The balance of capacity

- Capacity can either lead or lag demand.

- Inventory can be used to smooth out the peaks.

- Spare capacity can be used to supply other operations.

- The danger of this is that the original operation may receive a lower level of service.

CHAPTER 7

LAYOUT AND FLOW

Key questions
• What are the basic layout types used in operations?
• What type of layout should an operation choose?
• What is layout design trying to achieve?
• How should each basic layout type be designed in detail?

Topics covered
• The procedure by which operations finalize the detailed design of their layouts.
• The nature of the basic layout types: (a) fixed position layout; (b) process layout; (c) cell layout; and (d) product layout.
• The volume-variety characteristics of the basic layout types.
• The advantages and disadvantages of each basic layout type and the fixed and variable cost characteristics of each.
• The detailed design techniques which can be used to design each basic layout type.

Summary
What are the basic layout types used in operations?
• There are four basic layout types: (a) fixed position layout; (b) process layout; (c) cell layout; and (d) product layout.

What type of layout should an operation choose?
• Partly this is influenced by the nature of the process type, which in turn depends on the volume-variety characteristics of the operation.
• Partly also the decision will depend on the objectives of the operation. Cost and flexibility are particularly affected by the layout decision.
• The fixed and variable costs implied by each layout differ such that in theory one particular layout will have the minimum costs for a particular volume level. However, in practice, uncertainty over the real costs involved in layout make it difficult to be precise on which is the minimum cost layout.

What is layout design trying to achieve?
• In addition to the conventional operations objectives which will be influenced by the layout design factors of importance include the length and clarity of customer material or information flow, inherent safety to staff and/or customers, staff comfort, accessibility to staff and customers, the ability to co-ordinate management decisions, the use of space and long-term flexibility.

How should each basic layout type be designed in detail?
• Obviously this very much depends on the basic layout type chosen.
• For fixed position layout, the materials or people being transformed do not move but the transforming resources move around them. Techniques such as resource location analysis can be used to minimise the costs and or inconvenience of flow of the transforming resources around the transformed resources.
• In process layout all similar transforming resources are grouped together within the operation. The detailed design task is usually (though not always) to minimise the distance travelled by the transformed resources through the operation. Either manual or computer-based methods can be used to devise the detailed design.

• In cell layout the resources needed for a particular class of product are grouped together in some way. The detailed design task is to group the products or customer types such that convenient cells can be designed around their needs. Techniques such as production flow analysis can be used to allocate products to cells.

• In product layout the transforming resources are located in a sequence specifically for the convenience of product or product types. The detailed design of product layouts includes a number of decisions such as the cycle time to which the design must conform, the number of stages in the operation, the way tasks are allocated to the stages in the line, and the arrangement of the stages in the line. The cycle time of each part of the design together with the number of stages is a function of where the design lies on the 'long-thin' to 'short-fat' spectrum of arrangements. This position affects costs, flexibility, robustness and staff attitude to work. The allocation of tasks to stages is called line balancing, which can be performed either manually or through computer-based algorithms.

The facilities layout design procedure

Points to make

1 Laying out an operation is concerned with deciding where to locate transforming resources.

In this context transforming resources include facilities, machines, equipment and people.

2 Layout is important because it determines how the transformed resources (materials, information, customers) flow through the operation.

Layout affects the 'shape' of the operation, its appearance, cost and general effectiveness.

3 Operations managers face a double pressure. Having the wrong layout can be as expensive as changing it.

Changing a layout involves moving large resources and hence is not a task that you would want to repeat often.

Changing an existing layout disrupts the smooth running of the operation and can lead to lost production and/or customer dissatisfaction.

If an operation's layout is wrong work flow will be confusing, inventories will build up, processing times will extend and flexibility will be lost.

4 In theory layout is simple.

The layout procedure consists of four steps:

• Make sure you understand what the firm is trying to do - its strategic objectives.

• Select the appropriate type of process - largely dictated by volume-variety characteristics.

• Select the basic layout - options include fixed position, process layout, cell layout and product layout. This decision is not totally deterministic. You cannot say: 'we have adopted process type x, therefore we need layout type y'.

• Do the detailed design of the layout - produce the specification.

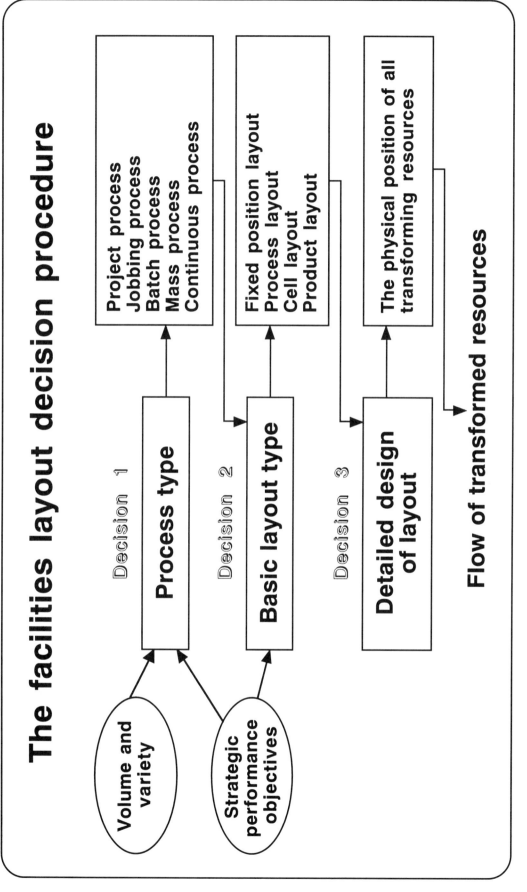

The facilities layout decision procedure

Volume and variety

Strategic performance objectives

Decision 1
Process type
- Project process
- Jobbing process
- Batch process
- Mass process
- Continuous process

Decision 2
Basic layout type
- Fixed position layout
- Process layout
- Cell layout
- Product layout

Decision 3
Detailed design of layout
- The physical position of all transforming resources

Flow of transformed resources

OHP37

The nature of the basic layout types

Points to make

1   There are four basic types of layout - fixed position, process, cell and product.

2   **The characteristics of the fixed position layout are:**
The transforming, rather than the transformed resources move. The reason for this is that the transformed resources may:

   • object to being moved;

   • be too delicate to be moved;

   • be too big to be moved.

The fixed position layout is vulnerable to disruptions in planning and control.

3   **The characteristics of the process layout are:**
The layout is designed to suit the needs of the transforming resources.

Similar processes are grouped together.

Products, information and customers flow from process to process according to their needs. The problem with this is that as different products, information and customers have different needs, the flow can be very complicated.

The density of flow is an important criterion for layout design. Different layouts will lead to different densities of flow.

4   **The characteristics of the cell layout are:**
The layout is arranged so that groups (families) of transformed resources can be processed in a single area. After being processed in one cell, the transformed resources may move to another cell for further processing.

The actual layout can be based around products or processes. The key to cellular layout is that it seeks to build on the best of both product and process layout thereby enhancing the flexibility of the operation.

5   **The characteristics of the product layout are:**
Transforming resources are located entirely for the benefit of transformed resources. This leads to a simple flow which is easy to control, but requires highly standardized products.

6   **Pure layouts are rare.**
More commonly mixed layouts, or different types of pure layout in different parts of the operation, will be found.

The nature of the basic layout types

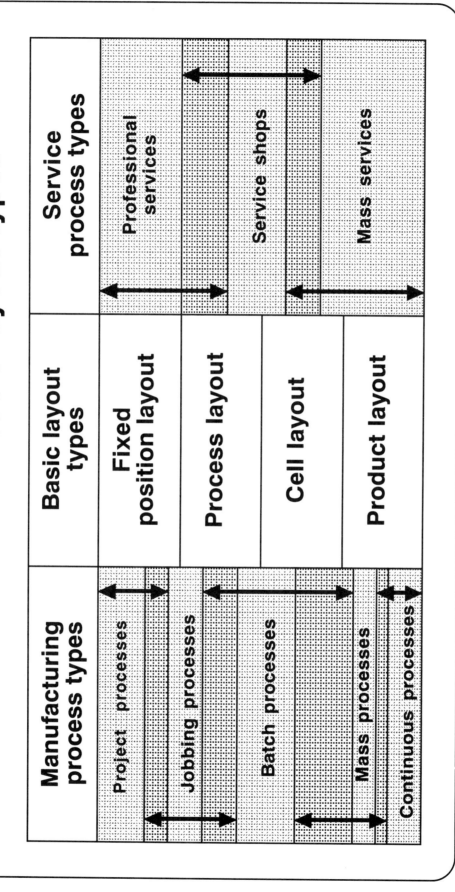

Manufacturing process types	Basic layout types	Service process types
Project processes	Fixed position layout	Professional services
Jobbing processes	Process layout	
Batch processes	Cell layout	Service shops
Mass processes	Product layout	Mass services
Continuous processes		

OHP38

The volume-variety characteristics of the basic layout types

Points to make

1   The flow of materials, information or customers through an operation depends on the layout adopted.

2   The importance of flow depends on the volume-variety characteristics of the operation.
Simple flows are both desirable and achievable for operations with high volumes and low variety.

Simple flows are desirable, but rarely achievable for operations with low volumes and high variety.

Basically as volume increases it becomes more important to get the flow right. As variety increases it becomes less feasible to get a simple flow.

3   The volume-variety characteristics of an operation tend to narrow down the choice of layout to one or two types.

Volume-variety characteristics

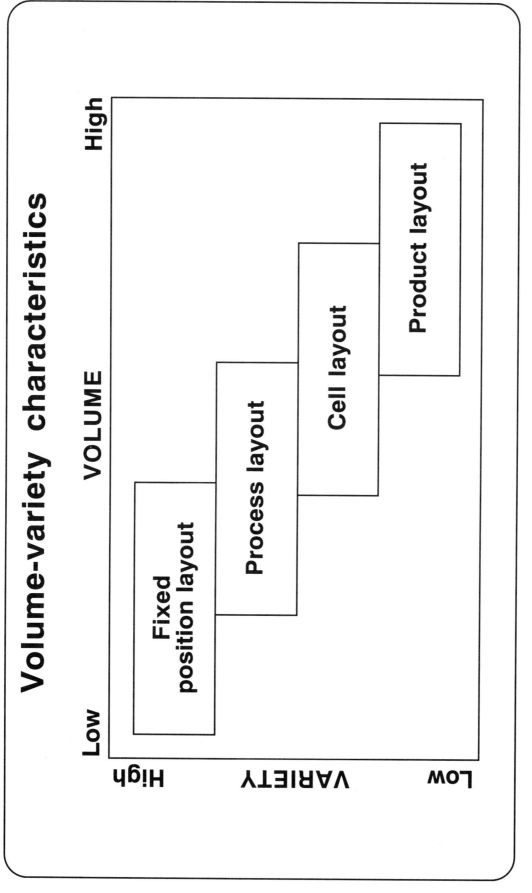

OHP39

The advantages and disadvantages of the basic layout types

Points to make

1 Each type of layout has some 'generic' advantages and disadvantages.

Advantages of fixed position layout: (a) very high product and mix flexibility; (b) product or customer not moved or disturbed; and (c) high variety of tasks for staff.

Disadvantages of fixed position layout: (a) very high unit costs; (b) scheduling of space and activities can be difficult; and (c) can mean much movement of plant and staff.

Advantages of process layout: (a) high product and mix flexibility; (b) relatively robust in the case of disruptions; and (c) relatively easy to supervise equipment or plant.

Disadvantages of process layout: (a) low facility utilization; (b) can have very high work-in-progress or customer queueing; and (c) complex flow can be difficult to control.

Advantages of cell layout: (a) can give good compromise between cost and flexibility for relatively high variety operations; (b) fast throughput; and (c) group work can result in good motivation.

Disadvantages of cell layout: (a) can be costly to rearrange existing layout; (b) can need more plant and equipment; and (c) can give lower plant utilization.

Advantages of product layout: (a) low unit costs for high volume; (b) gives opportunities for specialization of equipment; and (c) materials or customer movement is convenient.

Disadvantages of product layout: (a) can have low mix flexibility; (b) not very robust to disruption; and (c) work can be very repetitive.

2 Different fixed and variable costs are associated with each type of layout.

In fixed position layouts fixed costs are low and variable costs per unit of output are high.

In fact as you move from fixed position to product layouts, fixed costs tend to increase and variables costs tend to decrease.

3 Deciding which the lowest cost layout is for a given operation is not always easy as the costs have to be forecast.

Advantages and disadvantages

	Fixed position layout	Process layout	Cell layout	Product layout
Advantages	Very high product and mix flexibility. Product/customer not moved. High variety of tasks for staff.	High product and mix flexibility. Relatively robust in the case of disruptions. Easy to supervize.	Can give good compromise. Fast throughput. Group work can result in good motivation.	Low unit costs for high volume. Opportunities for specialization of equipment.
Disadvantages	Very high unit costs. Scheduling space and activities can be difficult.	Low utilization. Can have very high WIP. Complex flow.	Can be costly to rearrange existing layout. Can need more plant.	Can have low mix flexibility. Not very robust to disruption. Work can be very repetitive.

Detailed design techniques for each basic layout

Points to make

1 The purpose of detailed design is to operationalize the broad principles implicit in the choice of the basic layout.
A good layout will: (a) be inherently safe; (b) involve a short length of flow; (c) have a clear flow; (d) have good management co-ordination; (e) use space well; (f) be comfortable for the staff; (g) offer long-term flexibility; and (h) be accessible.

2 The output of the detailed design activity should be:
A specification which: (a) shows the precise location of all facilities, plant, equipment and staff; (b) details the tasks to be completed by each work centre; and (c) identifies the space to be devoted to each work centre.

3 Resource location analysis is one method of designing a fixed position layout.
Fixed position layouts seek to allow all the transforming resources to maximize their contribution to the transformation process by enabling them to provide an effective service to the transformed resources.

Resource location analysis involves looking at the needs of each resource centre and the importance of these needs. Based on this analysis a layout is designed.

4 Process layout is complex in that it is a 'factorial' problem.
If you have two processes there are 2! ways in which you can lay them out. If you have three processes there are 3! ways in which you can lay them out.

There are a number of tools and techniques that can be used to simplify the complexity which is inherent in the design of process layouts. These include: (a) common sense; (b) intuition; (c) trial and error; (d) heuristics - rules of thumb, including some that are computer based; (e) flow charts; and (f) relationship charts. Basically the objective is to try and reduce the distance that each transformed resource has to move.

5 Cell layout is a compromise between product and process layout.
When designing a cell there are two basic decisions that need to be made:
• The extent and nature of the cells - should the cells have their own indirect resources?

• Which resources should be allocated to which cell - should the cells be laid out according to the principles of product or process layouts? Should a special multi-purpose cell be set up to deal with the 'odds and sods'?

Product flow analysis (PFA) can be used to determine which products should be allocated to which cells.

6 For product layouts the nature of the design decision changes.
Product layouts are no longer concerned with where to put what, but what to put where.

Basically product layout involves addressing the line balancing problem by answering questions such as: (a) what cycle time is needed; (b) how can we cope with time task variation; (c) how can we balance the layout; (d) what shape should the line take; (e) how many stages are needed; (f) how should the stages be arranged; and (g) what work content should be given to them?

Detailed design techniques

- Fixed position - resource location analysis.

- Process layout - flow charts and relationship charts.

- Cell layout - product flow analysis.

- Product layout - assembly line balancing techniques.

CHAPTER 8

PROCESS TECHNOLOGY

Key questions
• What is process technology ?
• What are the significant materials processing technologies?
• What are the significant information processing technologies?
• What are the significant customer processing technologies?
• What are the generic characteristics of process technology?

Topics covered
• The relationship between product and process technology.
• Process technology developments in materials processing operations.
• Process technology developments in information processing operations.
• Process technology developments in customer processing operations.
• The three general 'dimensions' which are used to define all types of process technology: (a) its degree of automation; (b) its scale of operation; and (c) its degree of integration.

Summary
What is process technology ?
• Process technology is the collection of machines, equipment or devices which help operations transform materials, information or customers.
• This is different to the technology which is embedded in the product or service itself. However product technology and process technology issues do overlap especially in service operations.
• Operations managers do not need to know the technical details of all technologies but they do need to know, what does it do?, how does it do it?, what advantages does it give?, what constraints does it impose?

What are the significant materials processing technologies?
• Technologies which have had a particular impact include numerically controlled machine tools and machining centres, robots, automated guided vehicles, flexible manufacturing systems and computer integrated manufacturing systems.
• Each of these technologies can be seen as implying a different extent of integration between the four basic elements of designing, controlling, handling and managing materials.

What are the significant information processing technologies?
• Significant technologies include centralized and decentralized information processing including local area networks and wide area networks, electronic data exchange, the Internet and the World Wide Web. Of particular importance are the latter technologies which include the integration of computing and telecommunications technology.
• Within these information technologies are such developments as management information systems, decision support systems and expert systems

What are the significant customer processing technologies?
• There are no universally agreed classifications of customer processing technology as there are with material and information processing technology.
• The way we classify technologies here is through the nature of the interaction between customers, staff and the technology itself. Using this classification, technologies can be classified as those with no direct customer interaction, those with passive customer interaction and those with active customer interaction.

What are the generic characteristics of process technology?
• All technologies can be conceptualized on three dimensions. These are the degree of automation of the technology, the scale of the technology and the degree of integration of the technology.

The relationship between product and process technology

Points to make

1 All operations use some kind of technology and do so because they gain competitive advantage from it.
New technologies are being developed all the time, hence operations managers need to understand: (a) what emerging technologies can do; (b) what benefits they can provide; and (c) what constraints they might impose.

2 Process technologies are different to product technologies.
Process technologies include the machines, equipment and devices used by the operation to transform materials, information or customers.

Product technologies are those used in products or services.

It is easier to distinguish between product and process technologies in manufacturing operations than in service operations.

3 Operations managers have to manage process technologies.
To do this operations managers have to:

- be able to articulate how a given technology might improve an operation's effectiveness;

- be involved in the choice of technology;

- manage the installation and adoption of technology so it does not interfere with the ongoing activities of the operation;

- upgrade or replace technologies as appropriate;

- continually monitor the performance of the various technologies employed by the operation;

- integrate each technology into the rest of the operation.

As a result operations managers need to be able to understand:

- what a given technology does that is different from other technologies;

- how it does it - what its key characteristics are;

- what benefits it might provide;

- what constraints it might introduce.

4 The relative importance of product and process technologies varies depending on where a given product is in its life cycle.
Early in a product's life cycle product technology is important. Later process technology becomes more important.

5 Technologies are used in operations to process materials, information and customers.
Information technology has had a particularly major impact in recent years.

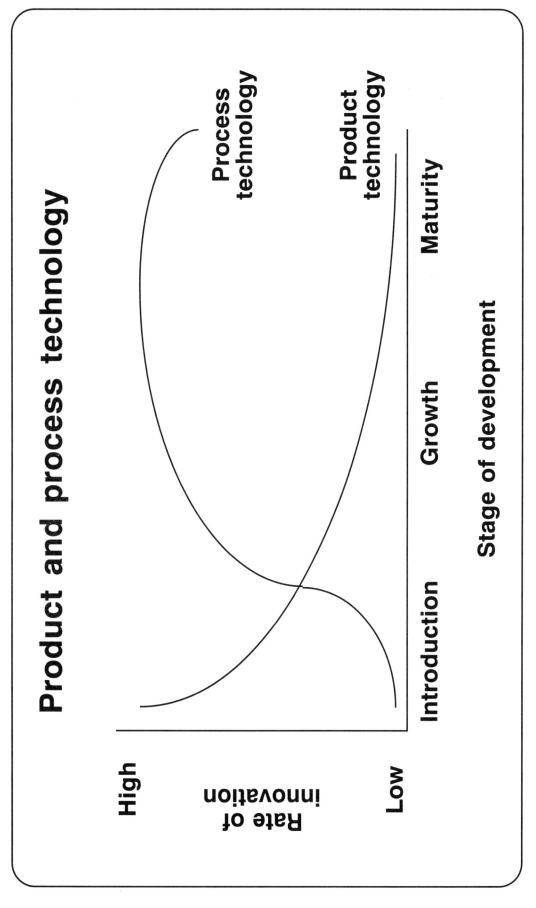

Product and process technology

Rate of innovation (vertical axis, High to Low)

Process technology

Product technology

Stage of development: Introduction — Growth — Maturity

OHP42

Process technology developments in materials processing

Points to make

1 Materials processing requires both technologies and tools.
Technologies used for materials processing include: (a) shaping; (b) forming; (c) cutting; (d) moulding; and (e) bending technologies.

Tools used for materials processing include: (a) lasers; (b) hard cutting tools; and (c) spark erosion.

2 The development of materials processing technologies can be traced from numerically controlled machine tools through to computer integrated manufacturing.

3 Numerically controlled machine tools use stored information to control production.
NC machine tools are accurate, precise, and can eliminate the need for skilled labour.

4 NC machining centres are an extension of NC machine tools.
NC machining centres have two features which NC machine tools lack. First, they have multiple degrees of freedom - hence a single NC machining centre can act as both a mill and a lathe. Second, they can cope with 'on-board' tool changes.

5 Robots became popular in the 1960s.
Robots are used for materials processing, handling and assembly. They have limited capabilities and are often used for things that are repetitive, monotonous, hazardous, and need doing for long periods without variation or complaint.

6 AGVs (automated guided vehicles) are used for transporting parts.
Transportation is a non-value added activity, hence many businesses seek to automate it. AGVs are small independently powered vehicles. They receive instructions from a central computer and are often guided by cables in the floor. AGVs provide cost advantages and can be a useful means of buffering work between operations.

7 Flexible manufacturing systems (FMS) build on the technologies already described.
An FMS usually consists of an NC workstation, loading and unloading devices, a means of transportation and a central computer. FMSs can best be described as self-contained micro operations with limited 'envelopes of capability'. They tend to be the most flexible automated technology, but are nowhere near as flexible as people.

8 The appropriateness of a given technology for a given operation depends partly on where the operation sits on the volume-variety continuum.

9 Computer integrated manufacturing (CIM) systems.
CIM systems seek to integrate many of the wider operations planning and control activities with the actual process of production.

Materials processing technologies

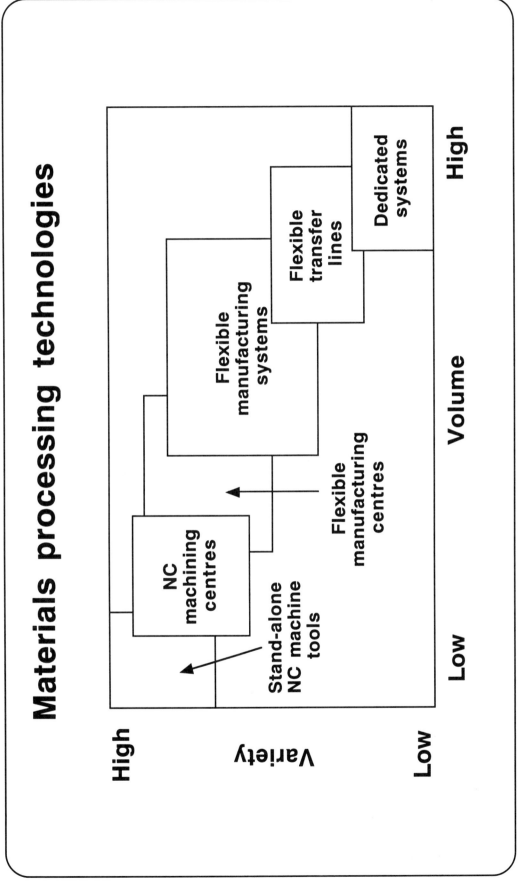

Process technology developments in information processing

Points to make

1   Information processing technologies have to collect, manipulate, store and distribute data.
The core of all information processing technologies is the computer which has been made highly accessible by the falling cost of computing power.

2   When computers were expensive, businesses used centralized information processing systems.

3   Now that computing power is cheaper, businesses use distributed information processing systems.
Distributed information processing systems, coupled with local area networks, have advantages in that they:

- provide local flexibility - computers can be added to or taken away from networks relatively easily;

- allow incremental growth;

- give operational autonomy;

- enable redundancy - make it easy to backup files;

- facilitate the use of shared resources - printers.

A major problem with distributed information systems is the difficulty of making computers 'talk to one another'.

4   In many applications telecommunications and information processing technologies are merging.
The digitalization of telecommunications transmissions has played a major part in this process.

An important industrial application of this 'new technology' is electronic data interchange (EDI). EDI can be used to eliminate paper and simplify the inter-firm order placement, order receipt, and payment processes.

Similar trends can be observed with the development of the Internet, the World Wide Web and intranets.

5   Another major development is the management information system (MIS).
Most businesses collect vast quantities of data on their performance. Management information systems are designed to manipulate these data and present them in a useful form. MISs are particularly useful in the planning and control process.

Specific types of MIS include Decision Support Systems (DSS) and Expert Systems (ES).

Information processing technologies

- Information processing technologies have to collect, manipulate, store and distribute data.

- Information processing technologies include computers and telecommunications.

- Increasingly these two technologies are becoming merged.

- Major industrial applications of this new 'integrated technology' include electronic data interchange (EDI), the Internnet, the WWW and intranets.

Process technology developments in customer processing

Points to make

1 Traditionally customer processing has relied on relatively low levels of technology.
Although services are generally provided by people, some customer processing operations are able to gain competitive advantage through technology.

2 The technologies used in the back office and the front office vary.
The back office is mainly concerned with information processing. The front office employs three different types of technology: (a) those which involve no customer interaction; (b) those which involve passive customer interaction; and (c) those which involve active customer interaction.

3 Technologies which involve no customer interaction.
Sometimes the service staff use technology on the customer's behalf. This is mainly done to reduce cost or save time.

4 Technologies which involve passive customer interaction.
Sometimes the customer comes into contact with the technology, but has no control over it. In such cases the customers are effectively the 'passengers of the technology'. A major concern here is safety.

Variety is usually low; customers are 'passengers of the technology'.

5 Technologies which involve active customer interaction.
Sometimes the main interaction during the service is between the customer and the technology. In these cases a major concern is training, as the customers have to be shown how to use the technology during the service process.

Key issues to be considered when designing technologies which require active customer interaction include:

- Complexity of service - the more complex the technology, the greater the need for training.

- Repetition of service - this is important for two reasons. First, if the technology is rarely used by customers it may not be worth the operation investing in training. Second, the more frequently the customer uses the technology the less likely they are to forget how to use it.

- Low variety - reducing task variety reduces the need for training.

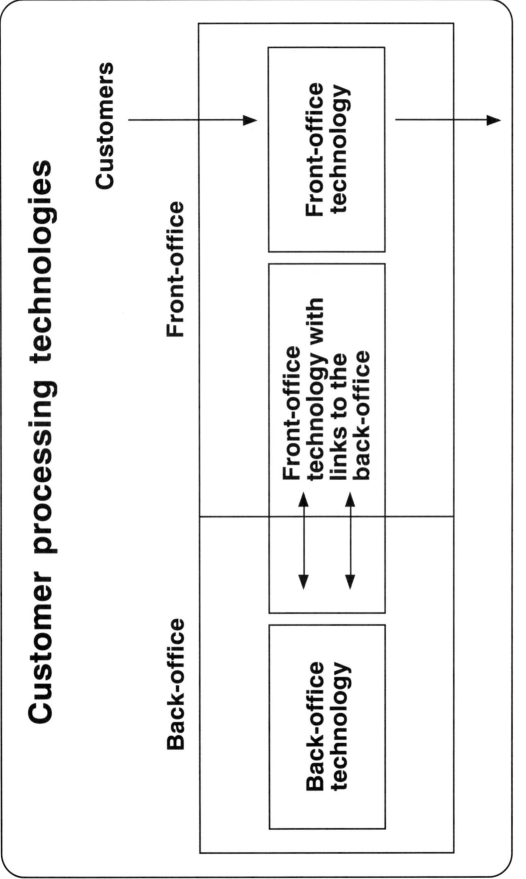

Customer processing technologies

Customers

Front-office

Back-office

Front-office technology

Front-office technology with links to the back-office

Back-office technology

OHP45

General dimensions used to define process technology

Points to make

1 Process technology comes in many forms which makes it difficult to generalize.

Having said this the degree of automation, the scale of the technology and the degree of integration are three dimensions that can be used to categorize technologies.

2 Technologies vary in their degree of automation.

The degree of automation of a given technology, or the capital intensity of the process, is defined by the ratio of technological to human effort required to operate it.

The benefits of high levels of automation are usually cited as savings in direct labour and reductions in variability. A number of other factors should also be considered, however:

• Can the technology perform the task better or safer than a human? Not just faster, but better in a broad sense? Can the technology make fewer mistakes, change over from one task to the next faster and more reliably, or respond to breakdowns more effectively?

• What support activities, such as maintenance or programming does the technology need in order to function effectively? What will be the effect on indirect costs, not just due to the extra people and skills which might be necessary but also the effect of increased complexity of support activities?

• Can the technology cope with new product or service possibilities as effectively as less automated alternatives?

• What is the potential for human creativity and problem solving to improve the machine's performance? Is it worth getting rid of human potential along with its cost?

3 Technologies vary in their scale.

Large-scale technologies often provide cost advantages through economies of scale.

Small-scale technologies are more flexible, have lower obsolescence risks and can be located exactly where they are needed. They also provide greater mix flexibility because they do not involve dedicating large units of capacity to particular products.

4 Technologies vary in their degree of integration.

A technology's degree of integration can be defined as the extent to which it seeks to link previously separate activities.

The advantages of a high degree of integration are that inventory is reduced, and that flow is simple, predictable and easy to control.

The disadvantages of a high degree of integration include expense and the fact that if part of the process fails the whole process may have to be stopped.

5 It is often worth considering methodology before technology.

Can the benefits the technology is supposed to bring be achieved by changing the methodology ? If so, is the technology really necessary?

Categorizing process technologies

- Process technologies can be categorized using three dimensions:

  - the extent to which they vary in their degree of automation;

  - the extent to which they vary in their scale;

  - the extent to which they vary in their degree of integration.

CHAPTER 9

JOB DESIGN AND WORK ORGANIZATION

Key questions
• What are the main decisions in job design?
• What are the main objectives of job design?
• What have been the significant influences on job design practice?
• How do the influences on job design differ?

Topics covered
• The elements which make up the job design activity.
• The objectives of job design.
• The advantages and disadvantages of using division of labour principles.
• The scientific management approach to job design including method study.
• The ergonomics approach.
• Behavioural principles of job design, including job enlargement and job enrichment.
• Autonomy and empowerment in job design.

Summary

What are the main decisions in job design?
• Job design involves deciding what tasks to allocate to each person in the organization and in what sequence to perform them, where to locate the job, who else should be involved in it, how people should interact with their workplace and their immediate work environment, what autonomy to give to staff and what skills to develop in staff.

What are the main objectives of job design?
• All job design decisions should attempt to devise jobs which engage the interest of staff, are inherently safe, give a reasonable quality of working life, as well as the more conventional objectives of operations - quality, speed, dependability, flexibility and cost.

What have been the significant influences on job design practice?
• Historically the first influence was the concept of the division of labour. This involves taking a total task and dividing it into separate parts, each of which can be allocated to a different individual to perform. The advantages of this are largely concerned with reducing costs. However, highly divided jobs are monotonous and, in their extreme form, contribute to physical injury.
• Scientific management took some of the ideas of the division of labour but applied them more systematically. The area of work study (divided into method study and work measurement) is most often associated with the scientific management. Although scientific management in its original form has fallen out of favour, new forms in which staff themselves perform method study analyses have been successfully applied more recently.
• Ergonomics is concerned primarily with the physiological aspects of job design. This includes both the study of how the human body fits into its workplace and how humans react to their immediate environment, especially its heating, lighting and noise characteristics.
• Behavioural models of job design are more concerned with individuals' reactions and attitudes to their jobs. It is argued that jobs which are designed to fulfil people's needs for self-esteem and personal development are more likely to result in satisfactory work performance.
• More recently the empowerment principle of job design has concentrated on increasing the autonomy which individuals have to shape the nature of their own jobs.

How do the influences on job design differ?

• The major difference lies in the relative balance between the two concepts of *control* of the job and the commitment of the staff performing the job. The chronological progression of influences on job design from division of labour through to empowerment are broadly in line with the movement from an emphasis on managerial control to an emphasis on the commitment and engagement of staff.

The elements which make up the job design activity

Points to make

1 Job design is very important for operations because operations contains the bulk of an organization's human resources.
Job design is important because:

- It defines the way people go about their working lives.

- It shapes their expectations of what is required.

- It influences their perception of how they contribute.

- It helps develop the organization's culture - the shared values, beliefs and assumptions.

2 Job design involves a set of decisions.

3 Job design involves deciding what tasks should be allocated to each person.
Doing the same task over and over again becomes monotonous. Giving each person a wide variety of tasks requires multi-skilling.

4 Job design involves deciding what sequence tasks should be performed in.
Sometimes this is defined by the design of the product. When it is not, it is often useful to sequence the tasks so that mistakes cannot be made.

5 Job design involves deciding where the job should be located.
Often jobs can be done in more than one place. Different locations can mean different task allocations.

6 Job design involves deciding who should be involved in the task.
Should the job be designed so that each person has a well-defined set of activities? Or should it be designed so that a group is asked to co-operate to complete a bigger set of activities?

7 Job design involves deciding how people should interface with facilities.
Inappropriate interfaces can reduce productivity and result in injury.

8 Job design involves deciding what environmental conditions should be established.
Performance can be affected by inappropriate environmental conditions.

9 Job design involves deciding how much autonomy each person should be given.
Should the person doing the job be allowed to change it? If so, what should they be allowed to change?

1 0 Job design involves deciding what skills need to be developed in the operation's staff.

The elements of job design

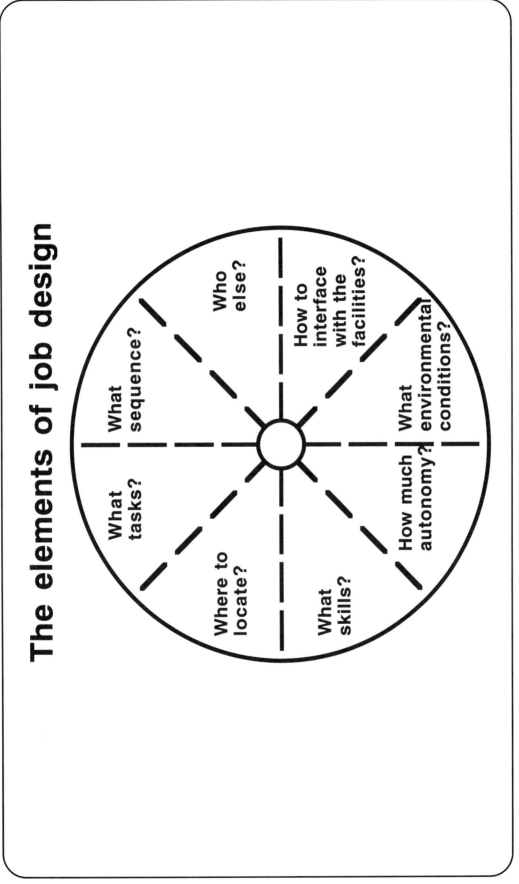

The objectives of job design

Points to make

1   **Appropriately designed jobs impact on the five performance objectives.**

2   **Quality:**
Well designed jobs mean that staff are less likely to make errors.

Furthermore giving staff autonomy means that they can change the job to make errors even less likely in the future.

3   **Speed:**
Well designed jobs enable staff to respond promptly - if required.

4   **Dependability:**
Well designed jobs can lead to staff being more dependable.

5   **Flexibility:**
Well designed jobs can enhance flexibility through multi-skilling.

6   **All elements of job design impact on productivity and therefore cost.**

7   **There are two other important objectives of job design.**
Health and safety - jobs must be designed so that they do not endanger the person doing the job, other staff in the operation, or customers.

Quality of working life - job design needs to take account of:

* job security;

* intrinsic interest;

* variety;

* opportunities for development;

* stress levels.

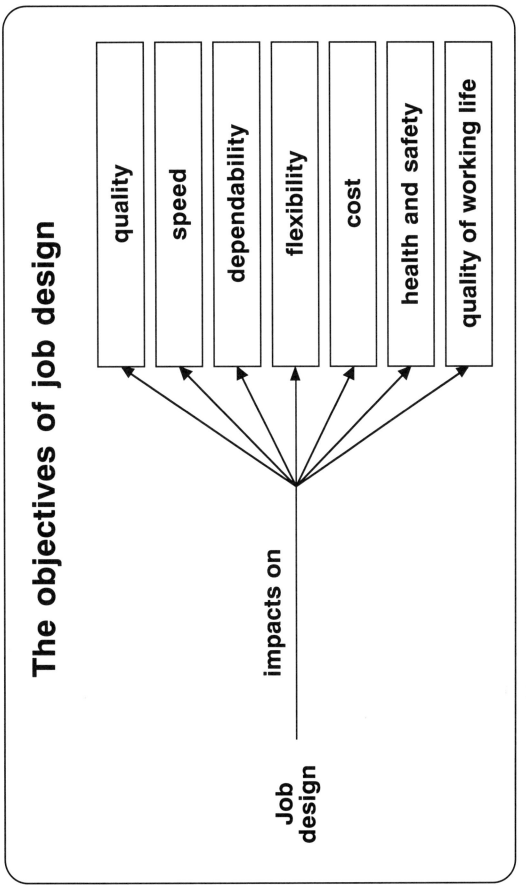

The objectives of job design

Job design

impacts on

- quality
- speed
- dependability
- flexibility
- cost
- health and safety
- quality of working life

OHP48

The division of labour principles

Points to make

1   Division of labour becomes an issue as soon as the operation is large enough to warrant the employment of more than one person.
Division of labour involves dividing the total task down into smaller parts, each of which is accomplished by a single person.

2   The advantages of the division of labour.
It promotes faster learning.

It makes automation easier.

It ensures that non-productive work is reduced.

3   The disadvantages of the division of labour.
It leads to monotony.

It can result in physical injury.

It is not particularly robust - division of labour implies that materials (or people or information) pass between several stages. If one of these stages is not working properly the whole operation can be affected.

Division of labour principles

Advantages	Promotes faster learning.
	Makes automation easier.
	Ensures that non-productive work is reduced.
Disadvantages	Leads to monotony.
	Can result in physical injury.
	Is not particularly robust.
	Can reduce flexibility.

The scientific management approach to job design

Points to make

1 The basic tenets of the scientific management approach to job design are that:

All aspects of work should be investigated on a scientific basis to establish the laws, rules and formulae governing the best methods of working.

Such an investigative approach to the study of work is necessary to establish what constitutes a fair day's work.

Workers should be selected, trained and developed methodically to perform their tasks.

Managers should act as the planners of the work (analyzing jobs and standardizing the best method of doing the job) while workers should be responsible for carrying out the jobs to the standards laid down.

Co-operation between management and workers is based on the 'maximum prosperity' of both.

2 Two separate, but related, fields grew from the 'scientific management' school.

- Method study concentrates on determining the methods and activities which should be included in the jobs.

- Work measurement is concerned with measuring the time which should be taken for performing jobs.

Together method study and work measurement are known as work study.

3 Scientific management has been criticized because it is not particularly scientific.

4 Despite this scientific management has some valuable principles - notably, method study.

Method study is a systematic approach to job design rather than a set of techniques. It consists of a six-step process:

- Select the work to be studied - choose jobs which will give a high payoff if redesigned .

- Record the present method - record the sequence of activities, or the path of movement.

- Examine the facts.

- Develop a new method which: (a) eliminates parts of the activity completely; (b) combines elements together; (c) changes the sequence of activities to increase the efficiency with which they are performed; and (d) simplifies the activity to reduce the work content.

- Install the new method.

- Regularly maintain the new method.

The scientific management approach

Work study

Method study
Method study is the systematic recording and critical examination of existing and proposed methods of doing work, as a means of developing and applying easier and more effective methods and reducing costs.

Work measurement
The application of techniques designed to establish the time for a qualified worker to carry out a specified job at a defined level of performance.

The ergonomics approach to job design

Points to make

1 The ergonomics approach is primarily concerned with the physiological aspects of job design.
There are two aspects to this:

- how the person interfaces with the physical aspects of his or her workplace;

- how the person interfaces with the environmental conditions prevalent in his or her immediate working area.

2 Two themes permeate the ergonomics approach.
The first is that there must be a fit between people and the jobs they do. This means either that people have to be made to fit jobs or jobs have to be made to fit people.

The second is data collection - ergonomics really is a scientific approach to job design.

3 Ergonomics workplace design seeks to understand how workplaces affect performance, fatigue, physical strain and injury.
To do this anthropometric and neurological aspects have to be considered.

Anthropometry explores issues related to people's size, shape and other physical attributes (strength, left-handedness). Anthropometric data, describing what 95% of the population should be able to do, fit under, reach for, etc., are available.

Neurology explores how people's sensory capabilities are engaged when interfacing with their working environments.

4 Environmental design seeks to understand how the immediate environment influences performance.
Key issues include:

- Working temperature - the comfortable temperature range will depend upon the type of work being carried out. Lighter work requires higher temperatures than heavier work.

  The effectiveness of people performing vigilance tasks reduces at temperatures above 29 degrees centigrade.

  The chances of accidents occurring increase at temperatures which are above or below the comfortable range for the work involved.

- Illumination levels - delicate jobs require high levels of illumination.

- Noise levels - intermittent and unpredictable noises are more disruptive than steady-state noise at the same level.

  High frequency noise (above about 2000Hz) usually produces more interference with performance than low frequency noise.

  Noise is more likely to affect the error rate (quality) of work rather than the rate of working.

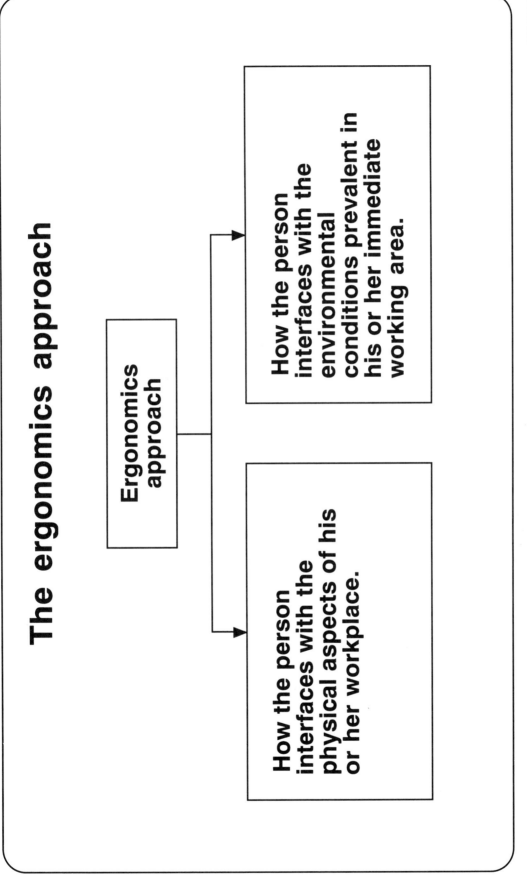

The ergonomics approach

Ergonomics approach

How the person interfaces with the physical aspects of his or her workplace.

How the person interfaces with the environmental conditions prevalent in his or her immediate working area.

The behavioural approach to job design

Points to make

1   The behavioural approach to job design is concerned with motivation theory and how it can contribute to job design.
The behavioural approach is based on the assumption that job design needs to take into account the need for people to gain something positive out of their work.

2   The behavioural approach does not assume a direct correlation between job design and performance.
Instead it assumes that well designed jobs lead to higher levels of motivation, which lead to better performance.

3   The basic principles of the behavioural approach.
People should be allowed to feel personally responsible for an identifiable and meaningful portion of work.

People should be provided with a set of tasks which are intrinsically meaningful or worthwhile.

People should be provided with feedback about the effectiveness of their performance.

4   There are various ways in which this can be achieved.
Options include: (a) combining tasks - increasing the number of separate elements or activities allocated to individuals; (b) forming natural work units - putting together activities which make a coherent whole; (c) establishing client relationships - encouraging staff to make contact with their internal customers; (d) vertical loading - making job holders responsible for 'indirect' activities such as scheduling and maintenance.; and (e) opening feedback channels - not only feedback from internal customers, but also feedback concerning the job holder's overall performance.

5   Hackman and Oldham introduced a useful concept - mental states.
Hackman and Oldham suggested that there are three mental states and that these are to do with: (a) how meaningful a person finds a job; (b) how much responsibility and control a person feels he or she has over the way the job is done; and (c) how much a person understands the results of his or her efforts.

The theory is that performance, defined in terms of motivation, quality of work, turnover and absenteeism, will be enhanced if high levels are achieved in all mental states.

6   Concepts related to the behavioural approach include:
• Job rotation - where individuals are moved periodically through different sets of tasks to provide some variety. This can increase flexibility and reduce monotony, but often disrupts work flow.

• Job enlargement - where extra tasks of the same nature are allocated to the individual. This does not make the job any more demanding, but does give greater variety and can give the job more meaning by making it more complete.

• Job enrichment - where individuals are given extra tasks involving more decision making and greater autonomy. This gives the job holder greater control over the job and provides more opportunities for personal development.

The behavioural approach

Techniques of job design	Core job characteristics	Mental states	Performance
Combining tasks	Skill variety	Meaningfulness of the job	Motivation
Forming natural work units	Task identity		Quality of work
Establishing client relationships	Task significance	Responsibility and control over the way the job is done	Turnover
Vertical loading	Autonomy		
Opening feedback channels	Feedback	Level of understanding of the results of efforts	Absenteeism

OHP52

Autonomy and empowerment in job design

Points to make

1   Empowerment is an extension of the concept of autonomy.

Autonomy means giving staff the ability to change how they do their jobs. Empowerment means giving the staff the authority to make changes to the job itself, as well as the way it is performed.

2   There are several benefits of empowerment.

These are:
- Faster on-line responses to customer needs.
- Faster on-line responses to dissatisfied customers.
- Employees feel better about their jobs.
- Employees will interact with customers with more enthusiasm.
- Empowered employees can be a useful source of information.
- It promotes 'word-of-mouth' advertising and customer retention.

3   There are also costs associated with empowerment

These are:
- Larger selection and training costs.
- Slower or inconsistent training.
- Violation of equity of service and perceived fair play.
- 'Give-aways' and bad decisions made by employees.

4   A related development is autonomous work teams

Autonomous work teams (or self-managed work teams) involve staff, often with overlapping skills, collectively performing a defined task with a high degree of discretion over how they actually carry out the task.

5   Not all autonomous work teams are successful

Problems occur when:
- Unclear objectives are given to teams.
- Certain individuals do not want to adopt team values and behaviour.
- Teams are seen as a 'quick fix' by management rather than thought through.
- Teams are not integrated with other parts of the operation so reinforcing interdepartmental separation.

6   The various approaches to job design have not replaced each other.

Initially the focus was on control (scientific management), then it moved to commitment (ergonomics and behavioural approaches). Empowerment moves the focus back on to control (as well as aiming to ensure commitment). The difference is that empowered people control their own jobs.

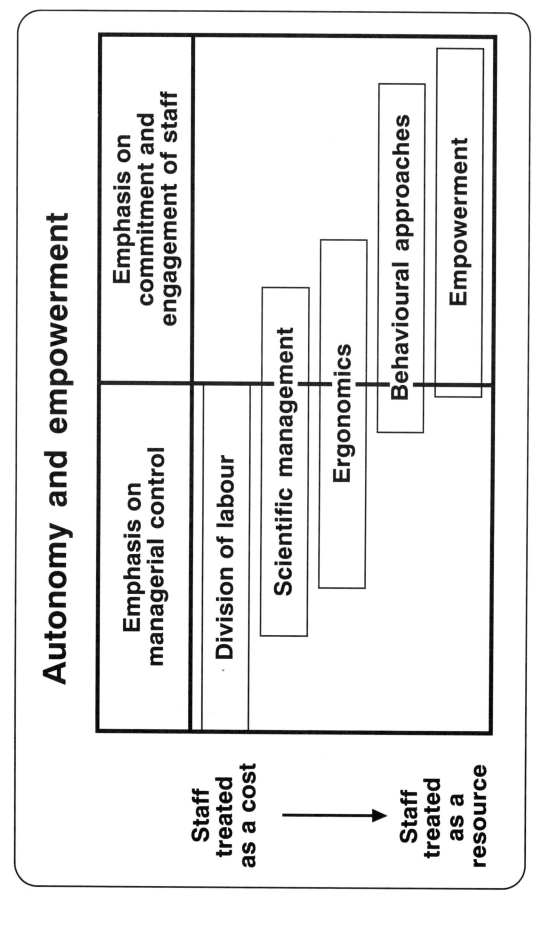

Autonomy and empowerment

Emphasis on managerial control	Emphasis on commitment and engagement of staff

Division of labour

Scientific management

Ergonomics

Behavioural approaches

Empowerment

Staff treated as a cost → Staff treated as a resource

OHP53

CHAPTER 10

THE NATURE OF PLANNING AND CONTROL

Key questions
• What is planning and control?
• What is the difference between planning and control?
• Why is planning and control important?
• How does the nature of demand affect planning and control?
• What is involved in planning and control?

Topics covered
• What is planning and control?
• Nature of demand and supply.
• Loading - finite and infinite loading.
• Sequencing - sequencing rules and their effect on operational performance.
• Scheduling - forward and backward scheduling, push and pull scheduling, constraint scheduling.
• The influence of volume and variety on planning and control.

Summary
What is planning and control?
• Planning and control is the reconciliation of the operation's potential to supply products and services with the demands of its customers on the operation. It is the set of day-to-day activities which runs the operation on an ongoing basis.

What is the difference between planning and control?
• A plan is a formalization of what is intended to happen at some time in the future. Control is the process of coping with changes to the plan and the operation to which it relates.
• Although planning and control are theoretically separable they are usually treated together.
• The balance between planning and control changes over time. Planning dominates in the long term and is usually done on an aggregated basis. At the other extreme, in the short term control usually operates within the resource constraints of the operation but makes intervention into the operation in order to cope with short-term changes in circumstances.

Why is planing and control important?
• Without consideration of planning and control activities operations would have no indication of what they were supposed to do or when they were supposed to do it, nor could they cope with deviations from what was expected.
• If planning and control activities are efficient and effective they should ensure that products and services are produced
    in the appropriate quantity
    at the appropriate time
    at the appropriate level of quality.

How does the nature of demand affect planning and control?
• The degree of uncertainty in demand affects the balance between planning and control. The greater the uncertainty, the more difficult it is to plan and greater emphasis must be placed on control.

• This idea of uncertainty is linked with the concepts of dependent and independent demand. Dependent demand is relatively predictable because it is dependent on some known factor. Independent demand is less predictable because it depends on the chances of the market or customer behaviour.

• The different ways of responding to demand can be characterised by differences in the P:D ratio of the operation. The P:D ratio is the ratio of total throughput time of goods or services to demand time.

What is involved in planning and control?

• In planning and controlling the volume and timing of activity in operations three distinct activities are necessary:

> **loading**, which dictates the amount of work which is allocated to each part of the operation.

> **sequencing**, which decides the order that work is tackled within the operation.

> **scheduling**, which determines the detailed timetable of activity and when activities are started and finished.

• Control can be classified as push or pull control. Pull control is a system whereby demand is triggered by requests from a work centre (i.e. an internal customer).Push control is a centralized system whereby control (and sometimes planning) decisions are issued to work centres which are then required to perform the task and supply the next work station.

• In manufacturing 'pull' schedules generally have far lower inventory levels than 'push' schedules.

• The volume and variety position of an operation has an effect on the nature of its planning and control. Customer responsiveness, planning horizon, the major planning decisions, the control decision and the robustness of planning and control are especially affected by volume and variety.

What is planning and control?

Points to make

1   Planning and control seeks to ensure that the operation runs effectively and produces what it should.

Good planning and control ensures that the organization's resources are used effectively and that the right quantity of goods or services is produced at the right points in time and with the right quality.

2   Planning and control is intimately linked to factory design.

The design of the operation determines what the operation is capable of doing. Planning and control determines what the operation actually does - i.e. whether the resources at the operation's disposal are used in a way that satisfies demand.

In fact planning and control is all about matching supply and demand.

3   The planning and control task is complicated by a number of factors.

Due to cost constraints organizations do not have infinite resources. Hence planning and control decisions have to be made about how limited resources should be deployed.

Physical constraints can also complicate the process. Even if an organization has infinite financial resources, the equipment it needs or the people it wants may not be available.

All products and services have a shelf-life. They have to be delivered while the customer still wants them. Such timing constraints further complicate planning and control.

Finally, products and services have to be manufactured so that they conform to certain quality standards. These quality constraints often have implications for the planning and control task.

4   Planning is different to control.

A plan describes what is intended to happen, but offers no guarantee that it will happen. A plan is a set of expectations based on experience, but as implementation proceeds unforeseen circumstances are likely to make it necessary to change the plan.

Control is all about coping with unforeseen circumstances. It is the process by which plans are modified so operations can still achieve their objectives, even though the assumptions made originally no longer hold.

5   The level of detail at which the planning and control activity is carried out varies over time.

Long-term planning and control usually has a financial focus and involves decisions being made at the aggregate level. Such decisions often have to be based on forecasts rather than hard data.

Medium-term planning and control is done at the partially disaggregate level and often includes 'contingency' planning.

Short-term planning and control is done at the fully disaggregate level. In the short term, time for a full evaluation of options is rarely available and hence the focus tends to be on responding quickly to unforeseen variation.

What is planning and control?

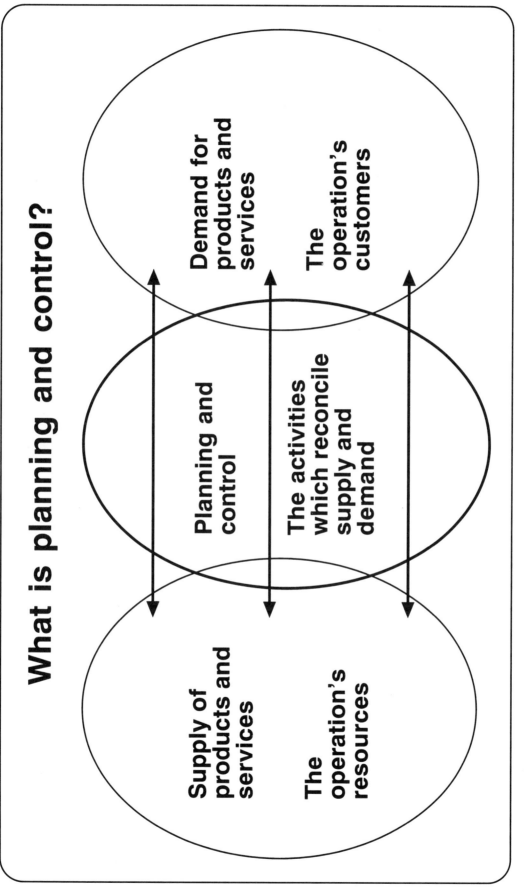

Demand for products and services

The operation's customers

Planning and control

The activities which reconcile supply and demand

Supply of products and services

The operation's resources

OHP54

The nature of supply and demand

Points to make

1 **The nature of supply and demand affects planning and control.**
Uncertain supply or demand, for example, means that contingency plans have to be developed.

2 **Demand can either be dependent or independent.**

3 **Dependent demand is predictable.**
It is based on known factors and makes forecasting straightforward.

4 **Operations with dependent demand either resource to order or make to order.**
Operations which resource to order allocate transforming and transformed resources only once the order has been received. A single order consumes a given set of resources and it is the order that triggers production.

Making to order is appropriate when the nature of demand is predictable (i.e. it is known that the order will be for a given type of product), but the timings and volumes are unknown. As with resourcing to order, the trigger which starts production is the receipt of an order.

5 **Operations with independent demand make to stock.**
When demand is independent and there is no forward visibility of orders operations have to forecast what they think future demand is likely to be. In such circumstances operations tend to make to stock. The risk of this strategy is that the operation may make too much, or too little.

In make-to-stock operations a single order tends to consume a fraction of the operation's resources.

6 **The P:D ratio provides another way of deciding whether an operation should resource to order, make to order or make to stock.**
P is the total throughput time - the time taken to purchase, make and deliver goods or services.

D is the time a customer is willing to wait between requesting a particular product or service and receiving it.

If P >> D the operation has to make to stock.

If P ≅ D the operation can afford to resource to order.

If P << D, and the product demanded is fairly standard, the operation can afford to make to order.

The actual P:D ratio is likely to vary from product group to product group, even within a given operation.

7 **The P:D ratio also provides an indication of the level of speculation within an operation.**
Forecasts are rarely perfect, but when P >> D, operations are forced to forecast. The greater the P:D ratio, the longer term, and hence the less precise the forecast will be.

The nature of supply and demand

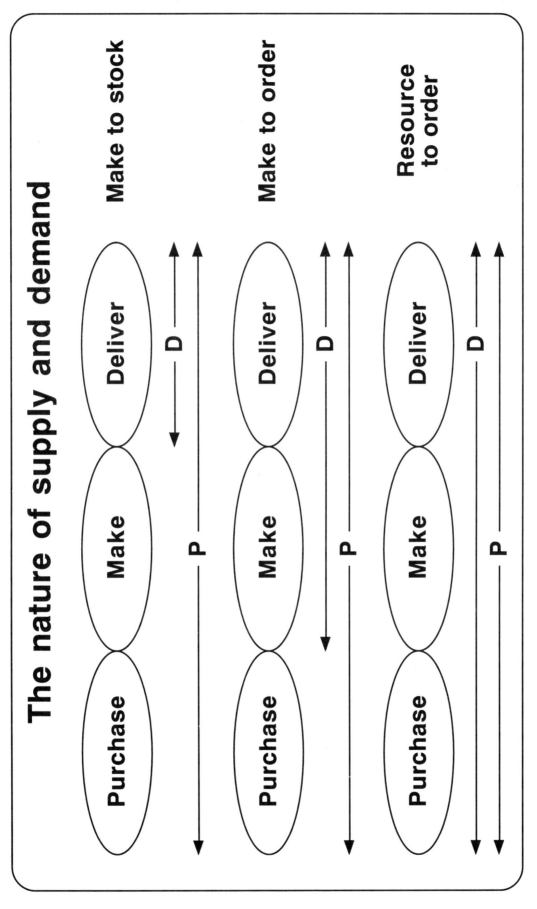

OHP55

Finite and infinite loading

Points to make

1 Planning and control involves reconciling supply and demand.
Three things have to be considered when reconciling supply and demand: scheduling, sequencing and loading.

2 Loading involves determining what volume of production the operation can cope with.
In theory machines can work for 168 hours per week. In practice weekends, set-ups and break downs mean there will be some periods when equipment is idle.

3 There are two basic types of loading: finite loading and infinite loading.

4 Finite loading is when work is allocated to machines only up to a certain set limit.
Finite loading is particularly relevant when:

- It is possible to limit the load - hospital appointments system.

- It is necessary to limit the load - for safety reasons you cannot have more than a predetermined number of people in an aeroplane.

- The cost of limiting the load is not prohibitive.

5 Infinite loading is when there is no limit to the work allocated to particular machines.
The assumption in infinite loading is that once the work has been loaded a way of coping with it will be found.

Infinite loading is particularly relevant when:

- It is not possible to limit the load - an accident and emergency department.

- It is not necessary to limit the load - a fast food restaurant.

- The cost of limiting the load is prohibitive.

6 Finite loading is extremely complex, particularly in a machine shop.
Finite loading involves complex calculations and the computing power required often prohibits it in machine shops.

Loading

Maximum time available

Normal time available | Not worked

Planned time available

Planned running time | Set-ups

Available time

Actual running time | Down time

OHP56

Sequencing

Points to make

1 Sequencing involves determining priorities.
When work arrives decisions must be made about the order in which jobs should be tackled.

2 Various 'sequencing rules' are used in operations.

3 Physical constraints.
The physical nature of the materials being processed may determine the priority of work.

Similarly the physical nature of the equipment used may determine sequence.

Sometimes the mix of work arriving at a part of an operation may determine the priority given to jobs. Therefore jobs that physically fit together may be scheduled together to reduce waste.

4 Customer priority.
Irrespective of when work arrives customer priority sequences it according to the size, or the importance, of the customer.

The problem with this rule is that it results in some customers getting very good service, while others get poor service.

5 Due date.
Sequence according to when the work is due.

This rule is flexible - urgent jobs get 'pushed' through the system - and usually improves delivery performance. It is not particularly efficient, however.

6 LIFO - last in, first out.
This rule is usually selected for practical reasons - loading an elevator.

It can have an adverse effect on delivery speed, however, and is often seen as inequitable.

7 FIFO - first in, first out.
Unlike LIFO, this rule is seen as equitable and can therefore be valuable in high contact operations.

The problem with sequencing on a FIFO basis, however, is that no account of urgency is taken and FIFO can result in poor service for some customers.

8 Longest operation time first.
Sequencing by longest operation time first leads to high utilization of work centres, but can result in low flexibility, long delivery lead times and poor delivery reliability.

9 Shortest operation time first.
Shortest operation time first is a good rule to use if the business is cash constrained as it ensures that quick jobs pass through the system rapidly.

The problem with sequencing by shortest operation time first, however, is that productivity may be reduced.

Sequencing

- Various sequencing rules are used in operations:

  - customer priority;

  - due date;

  - LIFO - last in, first out;

  - FIFO - first in, first out;

  - longest operation time first;

  - shortest operation time first.

Scheduling

Points to make

1   Scheduling involves deciding start and finish times for tasks.
Basically the scheduling activity involves producing a timetable.

2   Scheduling is complicated by the fact that it is a factorial problem.
Scheduling involves dealing with several different types of resource simultaneously. The number of possible schedules grows rapidly as the number of processing activities increases. The scheduling activity is further complicated by the fact that the schedule has to be recalculated when demand changes.

3   Gantt charts are a useful scheduling technique.
Gantt charts show:

- elapsed time as a horizontal bar;

- current time;

- job start and finish times.

Gantt charts are useful because they provide a visual representation of what is happening, and can be used to 'test' schedules.

4   Forward and backward schedules can be designed.
When forward scheduling, work is planned to start as soon as possible. This results in high labour utilization, increased flexibility and ensures that 'slack' is built into the schedule.

When backward scheduling, work is planned to start as late as possible. This reduces material costs, minimizes the operation's exposure and encourages a focus on due dates.

5   Schedules can be designed to push or pull work through the operation.
Push schedules usually rely on a central planning and control system. Each work centre completes all the work it can and pushes this work forward to the next work centre.

Pull schedules rely on the customer to pull work through the operation. When an order is received a product is dispatched from the stores. The 'gap' in the stores is the signal for assembly to produce a replacement product. The resultant 'gaps' in assembly are the signals for the machining centres to produce replacement components, etc.

It is now generally accepted that pull schedules tend to result in less inventory than push schedules.

6   Optimizing schedules is complex.
Johnson's Rule can be used to optimize schedules when there are only two machines in the system, but as the number of machines increases the likelihood of producing an optimized schedule decreases rapidly.

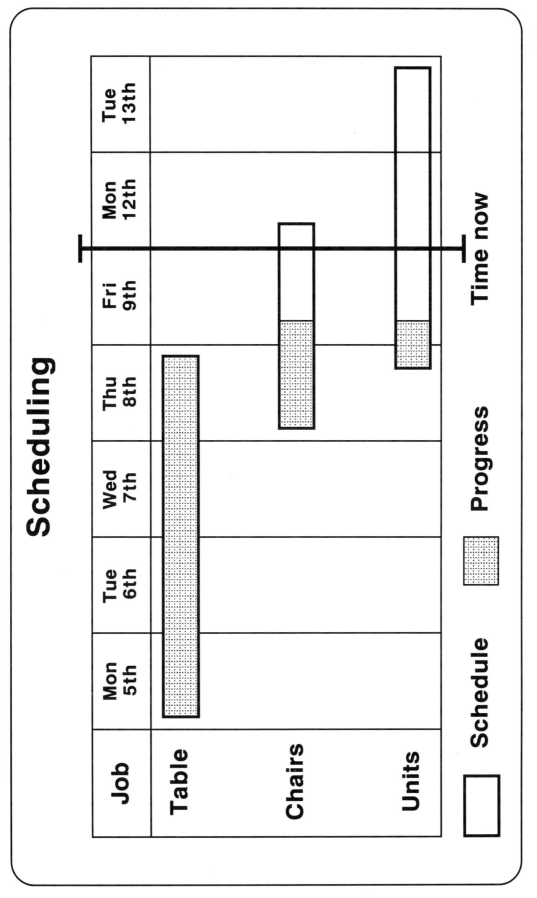

OHP58

Volume-variety influences on planning and control

Points to make

1 **The volume-variety characteristics of an operation have an impact on the type of planning and control systems that will be appropriate.**

2 **In operations with low volume and high variety the planning and control activity tends to focus on timing.**
There is little, or no product standardization.

Designs cannot be produced in advance of orders being received.

The time taken to respond to customers requests is usually long.

The requirements of the customer often 'emerge' during consultation.

There is little opportunity for forward planning.

3 **In operations with high volume and low variety the planning and control activity tends to focus on volume.**
Customers expect fast response.

The planning and control horizon can be long.

Process failures can have a major impact.

Volume-variety influences on planning and control

Volume	Variety	Planning horizon	Main planning decision	Control decision	Robustness
Low ←→ High	High ←→ Low	Short ←→ Long	Timing ←→ Volume	Detailed ←→ Aggregated	High ←→ Low

CHAPTER 11

CAPACITY PLANNING AND CONTROL

Key questions
• What is capacity planning and control?
• Why is capacity planning and control important?
• How is capacity measured?
• What are the ways of coping with demand fluctuation?
• How can operations plan their capacity level?
• How can operations control their capacity level?

Topics covered
• The nature of, and constraints on, capacity.
• The difference between long-term, medium-term and short-term aggregated capacity planning and control.
• The objectives of capacity planning and control.
• How capacity and demand are measured.
• The alternative ways in which organizations can reconcile capacity and demand.
• The use of cumulative representations and queuing theory to help capacity planning.
• The dynamics of controlling planning.

Summary
What is capacity planning and control?
• It is the way operations organize the level of value-added activity which they can achieve under normal operating conditions over a period of time.
• We normally distinguish between a long, medium and short-term capacity decision. This chapter deals with medium- and short-term capacity management where the capacity level of the organization is adjusted within the fixed physical limits which are set by long-term capacity decisions.
• This is sometimes called aggregate planning and control because it is necessary to aggregate the various types of output from an operation into one composite measure.

Why is capacity planing and control important?
• Because decisions made in capacity planning and control affect the ability to generate revenues and the extent of working capital required by the organization, as well as the normal operations objectives of quality, speed, dependability, flexibility and cost.
• Also because almost all operations have some kind of demand fluctuation (or seasonality) caused by some combination of climatic, behavioural, financial, social, political and festive factors.

How is capacity measured?
• Either by the availability of its input resource or by the output which is produced.
• Which of these measures is used partly depends on how stable the mix of outputs is. If it is difficult to aggregate the different types of output from an operation, input measures are usually preferred.
• The usage of capacity is measured by the factors 'utilization' and 'efficiency'.

What are the ways of coping with demand fluctuation?
• Output can be kept level, in effect, ignoring demand fluctuations This will result in under-utilization of capacity where outputs cannot be stored or the build-up of inventories where output can be stored.

• Chase demand by fluctuating the output level through some combination of overtime, varying the size of the work force, using part-time staff and subcontracting.
• Demand can be changed, either by influencing the market through such measures as advertising and promotion, or by developing alternative products with a counter-seasonal demand pattern.
• Most operations use a mix of all these three 'pure' strategies.

How can operations plan their capacity level?
• Representing demand and output in the form of cumulative representations allows the feasibility of alternative capacity plans to be assessed.
• In many operations, especially service operations, queuing theory can indicate the consequences of alternative capacity strategies.

How can operations control their capacity level?
• By considering the capacity decision as a dynamic decision which periodically updates the decisions and assumptions upon which decisions are based.
• By considering the major influences on which capacity strategies are adopted. The 'outlook matrix' which compares long-term and short-term outlook for demand (against capacity) is one way of doing this.

The nature of, and constraints on, capacity

Points to make

1 **Capacity is required to satisfy current and future demand.**

2 **There are two reasons why capacity is not simply an operations problem.**

   • The capacity planning process, which has a company-wide impact, requires inputs from all functions.

   • The capacity of each function's micro operations has to be matched to the capacity of the macro operation.

3 **Capacity planning and control is also known as aggregate planning and control.**

   Capacity planning and control is the highest level of planning and control. It does not distinguish between different types of product or service.

4 **Capacity has to be defined in terms of volume and time.**

   Capacity is the maximum level of value-added activity that the process can achieve under normal operating characteristics over a period of time.

   If time is not included it is impossible to establish what the processing capacity is.

5 **Operations often operate at levels which are below their maximum processing capacity.**

   This can be because of:

   • lack of demand;

   • a deliberate policy - having excess capacity enhances the operation's flexibility.

6 **Usually capacity is not balanced within an operation.**

   In most cases some processes will be under-utilized, while others will be operating at their ceiling.

The nature of aggregate capacity

- Aggregate capacity of a hotel:

    - rooms per night;

    - ignores the numbers of guests in each room.

- Aggregate capacity of an aluminium producer:

    - tonnes per month;

    - ignores types of alloy, gauge and batch variations.

Long-, medium- and short-term capacity planning

Points to make

1 **Capacity planning and control involves deciding how the operation should respond to fluctuating demand.**
In the long term, this can involve deciding whether to introduce, or 'delete', major increments of capacity.

In the short term, capacity planning and control involves making capacity decisions within the physical capacity constraints imposed by the operation's long-term capacity strategy.

2 **Medium-term capacity planning and control.**
  • Usually looks between two and eighteen months ahead.

  • Is based on forecasts of future demand and often involves changing the number of hours equipment is actually used.

3 **Short-term capacity planning and control is necessary because forecasts are rarely accurate.**
Hence short-term modifications to capacity invariably have to be made.

4 **One problem with aggregate capacity planning and control is that it assumes that the product mix is stable.**
This is rarely the case and different product mixes will have different capacity implications for the operation's different resources. This means that aggregate planning and control is never completely reliable, even in the short term.

Long-, medium- and short-term capacity planning

Macro operation with a given set of resources

might produce

6 tables

or

12 chairs

or

some combination

The objectives of capacity planning and control

Points to make

1 Capacity planning and control involves trying to minimize costs.

If capacity is greater than demand, resources will be under-utilized and unit costs will be high.

2 Capacity planning and control involves trying to maximize revenue.

If demand is greater than capacity the operation will be unable to satisfy some customers and revenue will be lost.

3 Capacity planning and control involves trying to minimize working capital.

If capacity is greater than demand and the excess capacity is used, work in progress, which the operation will have to fund, will build up.

4 Capacity planning and control involves trying to avoid quality problems.

If, for example, large fluctuations in demand are built into the operation's plan, temporary staff may have to be brought in which can lead to quality problems.

5 Capacity planning and control can increase speed.

The speed with which demand can be met can be increased by:

- building up inventory;

- eliminating queues by having sufficient capacity available at all times.

6 Capacity planning and control can improve dependability.

If demand is closely matched to capacity the operation will be less able to cope with unexpected disruptions and hence dependability will be reduced.

7 Capacity planning and control can enhance flexibility.

Flexibility is enhanced by surplus capacity.

8 The capacity planning and control process consists of three steps.

Step 1 - measure aggregate demand and capacity levels for the planning period.

Step 2 - Identify alternative capacity plans.

Step 3 - Choose the appropriate capacity plan for the circumstances.

Objectives of capacity planning and control

- Step 1 - Measure aggregate capacity and demand.

- Step 2 - Identify the alternative capacity plans.

- Step 3 - Choose the most appropriate capacity plan.

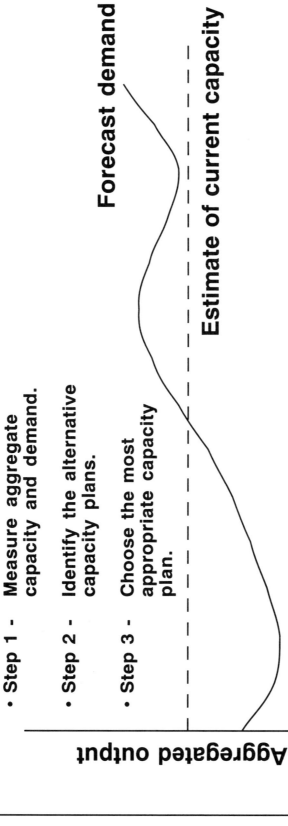

Forecast demand

Estimate of current capacity

Aggregated output

Time

OHP62

How capacity and demand are measured

Points to make

1 **Demand is usually forecast by sales or marketing.**
Forecasts need to:

- be expressed in terms that are meaningful for capacity planning and control;

- be accurate;

- give an indication of their relative uncertainty.

2 **Seasonality, of either supply or demand, causes major problems for forecasting.**
Seasonality can be annual, or weekly, or even daily (lunch time at the bank).

3 **The extent to which a company will have to cope with short-term demand fluctuations is a function of how long customers are willing to wait.**

4 **The major problem of measuring demand is that demand is inherently uncertain.**

5 **The major problem of measuring capacity is its complexity.**
Output is a function of product mix. Hence in operations where the product mix varies widely, it is better to measure capacity in terms of input.

6 **Input measures can be converted to output measures and vice versa.**
Often operations need to convert input measures to output measures and vice versa because capacity is usually expressed in terms of input, whereas demand is usually expressed in terms of output.

The conversion process can never be exact as it involves making certain assumptions.

7 **There is a difference between design capacity and effective capacity.**
Effective capacity is equal to the design capacity less any capacity lost through set-ups, scheduling changes, etc.

8 **Useful measures associated with capacity include efficiency and utilization.**
Efficiency is actual output divided by the effective capacity.

Utilization is actual output divided by the design capacity.

High utilization is not always desirable as it can lead to increased work in progress.

How capacity and demand are measured

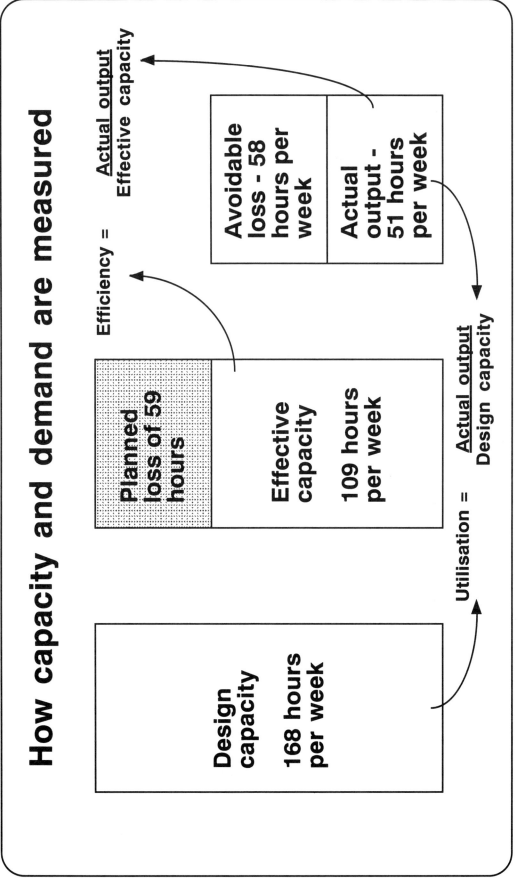

Design capacity

168 hours per week

Planned loss of 59 hours

Effective capacity

109 hours per week

Avoidable loss - 58 hours per week

Actual output - 51 hours per week

$$\text{Efficiency} = \frac{\text{Actual output}}{\text{Effective capacity}}$$

$$\text{Utilisation} = \frac{\text{Actual output}}{\text{Design capacity}}$$

OHP63

Ways of reconciling capacity and demand

Points to make

1 There are three pure ways in which an operation can reconcile supply and demand.

2 Level capacity planning - keep activity levels constant and ignore fluctuations in demand.

Level capacity planning involves employing the same number of staff and using the same processes so that a constant level of output is maintained.

It is only applicable to operations producing non-perishable goods, as it leads to the creation of inventory which has to be stored and which may become obsolete if the forecast is wrong.

The main benefits of level capacity planning are that it results in a stable employment pattern, high process utilization, high productivity and low unit costs.

3 Chase demand planning - adjust capacity levels to reflect the fluctuations in demand.

Chase demand planning is difficult to achieve in reality because it involves varying the hours people are asked to work and the amount of equipment the operation has.

Strategies to achieve chase demand planning include sub-contracting work, using part-time staff, varying the size of the workforce, ensuring that staff are multi-skilled and offering overtime.

Chase demand planning is unlikely to appeal to operations which are capital intensive or which produce standard, non-perishable products.

4 Demand management - attempt to change demand so that peaks in demand are moved to slacker periods.

Strategies for demand management include:

- Promotional activities - these attempt to encourage customers to place orders at 'off-peak' times.

- Introduce alternative products and services which smooth out the demand pattern. The problem with this strategy is that it may reduce the amount of attention management pays to the operation's core products or services.

5 Operations rarely pursue a pure strategy - generally they use mixed plans.

6 Yield management is useful for services.

Yield management is useful when an operation's capacity is relatively fixed, the market it serves can be segmented, the services it offers cannot be stored, the services it offers are sold in advance, and the marginal cost of making a sale is low.

Yield management strategies include: (a) overbooking; (b) price discounting; and (c) varying service types (e.g. offering first and second class tickets).

Ways of reconciling capacity and demand

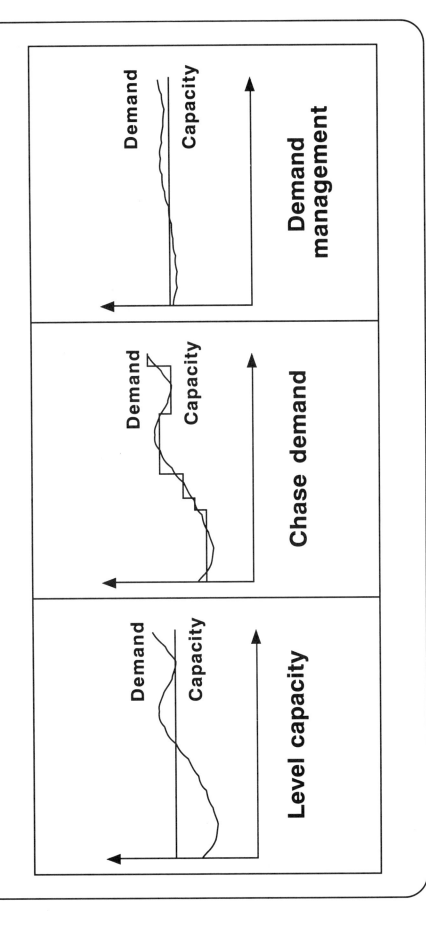

Level capacity

Chase demand

Demand management

Using cumulative representations to help plan capacity

Points to make

1   Cumulative representations of demand could be used to assess capacity availability.
If sufficient capacity is to be available to meet demand, then the cumulative capacity must always be greater than the cumulative demand.

2   Capacity is not constant in most operations.
This makes it difficult to calculate cumulative capacity.

3   Cumulative representations show predicted inventory levels.
Assuming that the operation aims to maximize utilization then the difference between cumulative capacity and cumulative demand at any point in time will be inventory.

4   Cumulative representations can be used to compare plans.
If an operation decides to adopt a strategy of chasing demand then it should, at least in theory, hold no inventory. The same operation, however, would incur costs associated with changing its capacity.

These costs would have to be reflected in the cumulative representation, if it were to be used to compare the chase demand strategy with other possible capacity strategies.

5   Queueing theory provides a useful model for services.
Services cannot be stored, hence cumulative representations are of little value.

Most services face two basic problems.

- They do not know when customers will arrive.

- They do not know how long it will take to serve a particular customer.

For services, capacity planning is really a trade-off between customer service and system utilization. If there are too many servers, costs will increase. If there are too few servers, queues will build up.

Queueing theory provides some tools and techniques which can be used to analyze this problem.

Cumulative representations

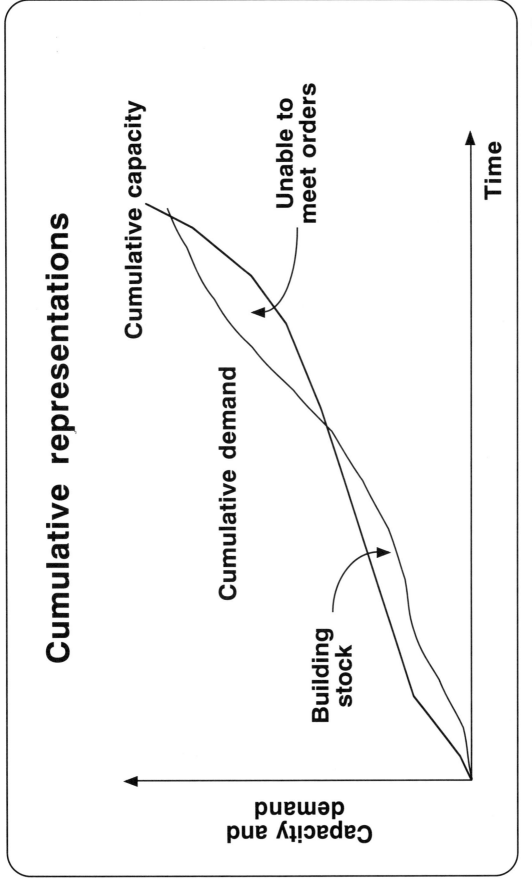

Cumulative capacity

Cumulative demand

Unable to meet orders

Building stock

Capacity and demand

Time

The dynamics of controlling planning

Points to make

1   Capacity management is a dynamic activity.
Capacity control involves changing actual capacity in response to actual demand.

2   The cost of changing capacity depends upon:
- the point from which the change is being made;

- the degree of the change;

- the direction of the change.

Generally capacity changes are cheaper if they are moving capacity towards the normal level for the operation.

3   A useful capacity control tool is the outlook matrix.
Outlook, which can be considered in both the long and short term, is defined as forecast demand over forecast capacity.

The outlook is said to be poor if forecast demand over forecast capacity is less than one.

The outlook is said to be normal if forecast demand over forecast capacity is approximately equal to one.

The outlook is said to be good if forecast demand over forecast capacity is greater than one.

If the outlook is:
- Poor, in both the short and long term - capacity should be reduced.

- Normal in the short term and poor in the long term - current capacity should be maintained and decisions about reducing capacity should be delayed.

- Good in the short term and poor in the long term - the operation faces a dilemma, because the extra capacity that is needed in the short term will be unnecessary in the long term. In this scenario the options include offering overtime or employing temporary staff.

- Poor in the short term and normal in the long term - capacity should be temporarily reduced or the idle time should be tolerated.

- Normal in both the short and long term - no action should be taken.

- Good in the short term and normal in the long term - capacity should be temporarily increased.

- Good in the long term - capacity should be increased irrespective of the short term position. In fact, if the short term outlook is poor the excess capacity could be used to build stock.

The dynamics of controlling planning

Short-term outlook

	Poor	Normal	Good
Poor	Layoff staff	Delay any action	Overtime
Normal	Short-time working	Do nothing	Overtime
Good	Make for inventory	Hire and make for inventory	Hire staff

Long-term outlook

OHP66

CHAPTER 12

INVENTORY PLANNING AND CONTROL

Key questions
• What is inventory ?
• Why is it necessary?
• How much inventory should an operation hold?
• When should an operation replenish its inventory?
• How can inventory be controlled?

Topics covered
• The role, position and types of inventories in operations.
• The order quantity decision and inventory costs.
• Economic order quantity (EOQ) type approaches and the criticisms of EOQ.
• The replenishment order timing decision for continuous and periodic review systems.
• Inventory control decisions, inventory classifications, measures of inventory and inventory control systems.

Summary
What is inventory ?
• Inventory, or stock, is the stored accumulation of the transformed resources in an operation.
• Sometimes the words stock or inventory are also used to describe transforming resources but the terms stock control or inventory control are nearly always used in connection with transformed resources.
• Almost all operations keep some kind of inventory, most usually of materials but also of information and customers (customer inventories are normally called queues)

Why is it necessary?
• Inventory occurs in operations because the timing of supply and the timing of demand does not always match. Inventories are needed therefore to smooth the differences between supply and demand.
• There are four main reasons for keeping inventory. These are:
     to cope with random or unexpected interruption in supply or demand - buffer inventory,
     to cope with an an operation's inability to make all products simultaneously - cycle inventory,
     to cope with planned fluctuations in supply or demand - anticipation inventory,
     to cope with transportation delays in the supply network - pipeline inventory.

How much inventory should an operation hold?
• This depends on balancing the costs associated with holding stocks against the costs associated with placing an order. The main stock holding costs are usually related to working capital whereas the main order costs are usually associated with the transactions necessary to generate the information to place an order.
• The most common approach to determining the amount of inventory to order is the economic order quantity (EOQ) formula. The EOQ formula can be adapted to different types of inventory profile using different stock behaviour assumptions.
• The EOQ approach, however, has been subject to a number of criticisms regarding the true cost of holding stock, the real cost of placing an order and the use of EOQ models as prescriptive devices.

When should an operation replenish its inventory?

• Partly this depends on the uncertainty of demand. Orders are usually timed to leave a certain level of average safety stock when the order arrives. The level of safety stock is influenced by the variability both of demand and lead-time of supply. These two variables are usually combined into a lead-time usage distribution.

• Using a re-order level as the trigger for placing replenishment orders necessitates the continual review of inventory levels. This can be time consuming and expensive. An alternative approach is to make a replenishment order of varying size but at fixed time periods.

How can inventory be controlled?

• The key issue here is how managers discriminate in the level of control which they apply to different stock items. The most common way of doing this is what is known as the ABC classification of stock. This uses the Pareto principle to distinguish between the different value or significance placed on types of stock.

• Inventory is usually managed through sophisticated computer-based information systems which have a number of functions. These are, the updating of stock records, the generation of orders, the generation of inventory status reports and demand forecasts.

Role, position and types of inventory

Points to make

1   Inventory or stock is the term used to describe the stored accumulation of material resources in a transformation system.
Normally the term inventory is used to refer to transformed resources, rather than transforming resources.

2   All operations keep inventory.
Supermarkets keep inventory on the shelves of their stores. Manufacturing operations keep inventory on the shop floor.

An important issue is how should inventory be valued. In theory, transformation processes add value to the input resources. In practice, as long as these resources remain unsold the added value is unrealized.

3   Operations hold inventory because of differences in the rate or timing of supply and demand.
If all items could be supplied exactly when they were demanded there would be no need to hold inventory.

4   There are different types of inventory.
• Buffer, or safety, stocks are used to compensate for the uncertainties inherent in supply and demand.

• Cycle inventories are used to compensate for irregularities in supply. Operations rarely have enough resources to produce their whole product range simultaneously and hence there will always be irregularities in supply.

• Anticipation inventories are used when product demand fluctuates, or supply is prone to disruption.

• Pipeline inventories are necessary because materials cannot be transported from one place to another instantaneously.

5   Operations can position inventories in different places.
Some operations choose to have a single stock of goods. Some choose to store inventories in two different places. Others choose to hold inventories in multiple locations.

The role of inventory

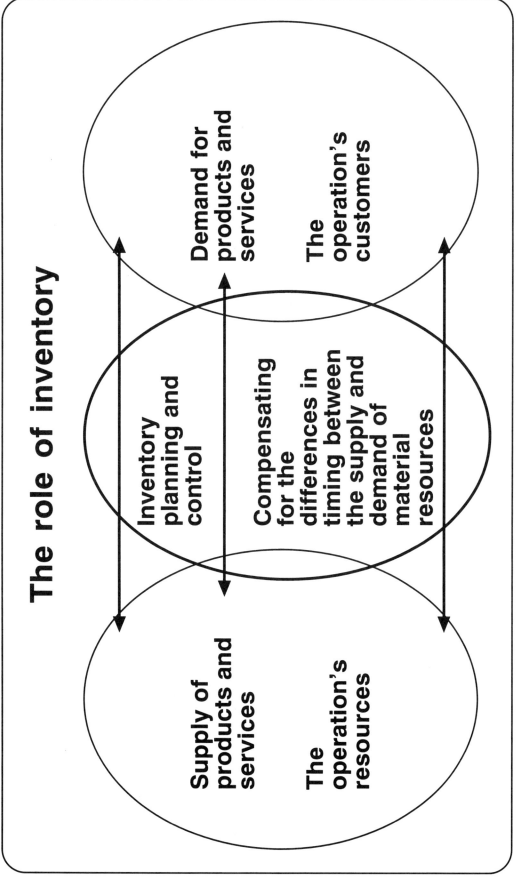

OHP67

The order quantity decision and inventory costs

Points to make

1   Inventory management involves three things:
- deciding how much to order;

- deciding when to order;

- deciding how to control the inventory.

2   Deciding how much to order involves a trade-off.
The volume decision involves balancing two sets of costs:

- the cost of holding stock;

- the cost of purchasing items.

Ordering small quantities reduces the capital tied up in raw materials, but increases the time and effort that has to be invested in placing orders.

Ordering large quantities makes frequent purchases unnecessary, but requires greater capital investment and larger storage facilities.

3   There are various types of inventory cost.
- price discount costs - buying in bulk often results in price discounts.

- stock-out costs - caused by failure to meet demand.

- funding inventory - operations usually have to pay suppliers long before they receive payment from their customers. Hence money, which has to be funded, flows out of the operation, long before revenue comes in.

- storage costs - inventory has to be stored, warehouses have to be heated and store keepers have to be paid.

- production inefficiency costs - inventory provides a buffer which protects the operation and hides its inefficiencies.

- obsolescence costs - whenever goods are stored there is always a danger that they will deteriorate, or become obsolete.

4   Inventory profiles provide a useful visual representation of inventory over time
Inventory profiles take account of:

- orders arriving;

- stock being used.

The order quantity decision

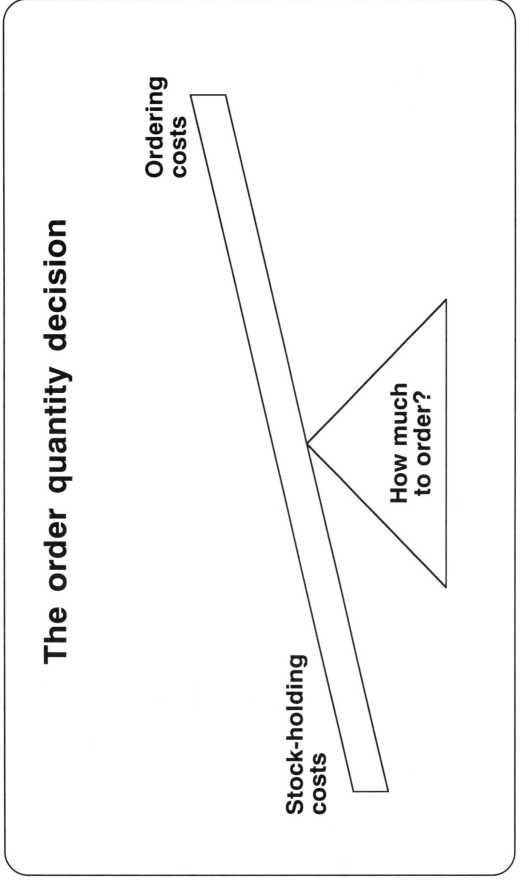

Ordering costs

Stock-holding costs

How much to order?

The economic order quantity

Points to make

1   The economic order quantity attempts to balance the advantages and disadvantages of holding stock.

The economic order quantity (EOQ) model takes account of:

- Holding costs - working capital, storage and obsolescence risks.

- Order costs - price discounts and costs of placing orders.

The rationale underlying the EOQ model is that, for any given set of circumstances, an order quantity, Q, exists that minimizes the total order and holding costs.

2   The EOQ is not particularly sensitive to small changes in Q.

To build an EOQ model various costs have to be estimated. As the EOQ is not particularly sensitive to small variations in Q, it does not matter if these estimates are not 100% accurate.

3   The EOQ assumes that the entire replenishment batch arrives at a single point in time.

Sometimes this is not the case, and in these circumstances it is better to use the economic batch quantity (EBQ) model.

The EBQ model, which is also known as the economic manufacturing quantity (EMQ) model and the production order quantity (POQ) model, takes account of the cost of back orders.

4   The EOQ has been subject to some criticism.

5   The assumptions underpinning the EOQ (stable demand, fixed and identifiable order costs and linear stock-holding costs) have been questioned.

The fact that the EOQ curve is relatively flat and hence insensitive to small changes in Q makes this less of a problem, but some of the assumptions in the model are inappropriate:

- Demand is not constant.

- Order costs are not fixed.

- Stock-holding costs are not linear.

6   The fact that the EOQ hides some of the real costs of stock has been recognized.

Inventory hides problems. This 'intangible cost' is not reflected in the EOQ.

7   The fact that the EOQ is used as a prescriptive model causes some concern.

The EOQ is really a descriptive model. Sometimes, however, it is used to provide a spurious justification for management decisions.

8   The EOQ does not encourage operations managers to ask 'how can I change this operation so that it needs less stock'?

The economic order quantity

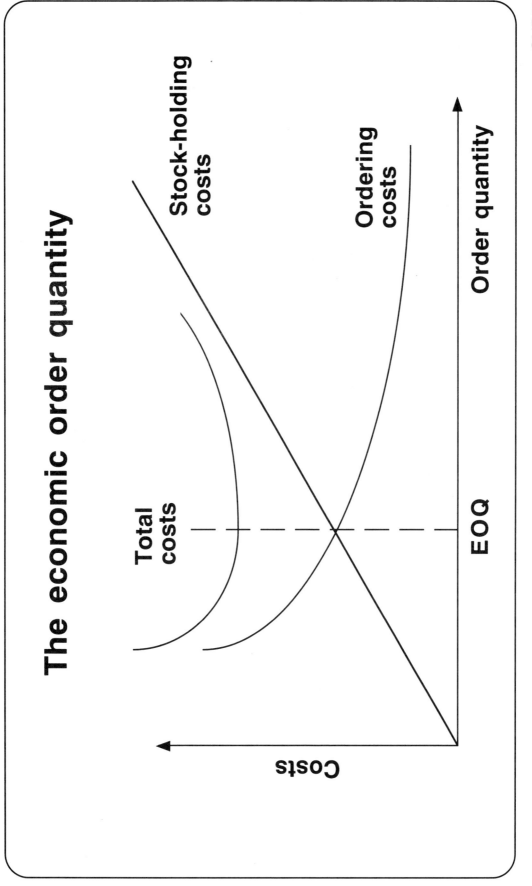

OHP69

The replenishment order timing decision

Points to make

1   The timing decision follows the volume decision.
The timing decision involves determining when an order should be placed.

2   A trade-off is associated with the timing decision.
Goods do not arrive instantaneously, hence orders have to be placed in advance of when they will be needed. If the order is placed too early the operation will have excess stock. If it is placed too late the operation will face a shortage situation.

3   The order placement process can be triggered by:
  • A time-based reorder point (ROP) system. This involves replenishment orders being placed just as the the stock falls to zero **minus** the order lead time.

  • A stock-based reorder level (ROL) system. This involves replenishment orders being placed when the stock falls to a certain level.

4   Pure ROP and ROL systems assume constant demand and order lead times.
In reality demand fluctuates and lead times vary, hence replenishment orders have to be placed slightly early.

On average this will result in extra (buffer or safety) stock.

The appropriate level of safety stock can be calculated by considering the probability of stock-out, the variability in lead times and the fluctuation in demand.

5   The ROP and ROL systems are based on a continuous review of the inventory position.
The major advantage of this is that order quantities can be kept constant and set at the EOQ.

The major disadvantage is that the timing of the orders will be irregular.

6   An alternative approach would be to adopt a periodic review system.
The periodic review system simply involves reviewing the inventory position at predetermined points in time and replacing any stock that has been used.

The major advantage of the periodic review system is its simplicity. Unfortunately it does not sit well with the EOQ, although the EOQ can be used to calculate ideal review frequencies.

7   Two and three bin systems.
These are simple visual methods which make inventory level tracking easy.

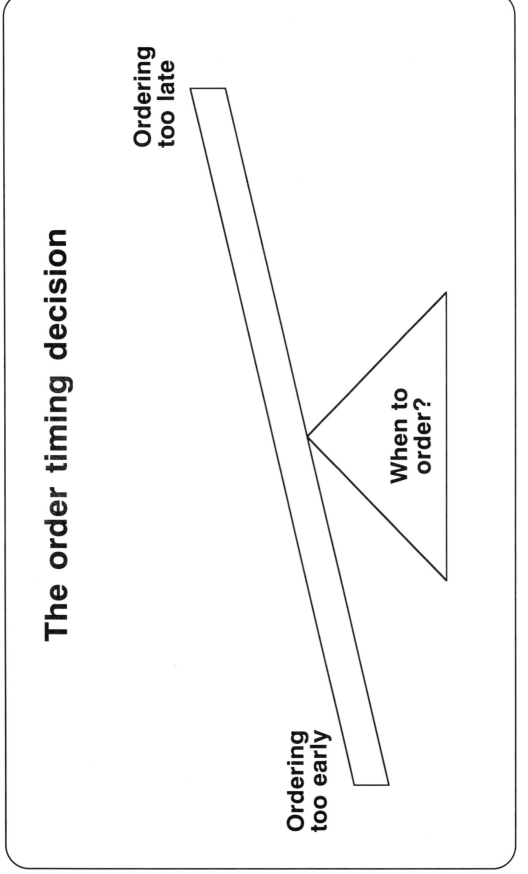

The order timing decision

Ordering too late

When to order?

Ordering too early

OHP70

Inventory classifications, measures and control systems

Points to make

1 Operations need to:
- be able to distinguish between different types of stock so that they can match the degree of control applied to a particular item with the importance of that item;

- invest in an information processing system to help them manage their inventories.

2 The ABC system for classifying inventory is a useful one.
Some items are more important than others. In the ABC classification system:

- Class A items include the 20% or so of high-value items which account for around 80% of the total stock value.

- Class B items include the next 30% or so of medium-value items which account for around 10% of the total stock value.

- Class C items include the remaining 50% or so of low-value items which account for around the last 10% of the total stock value.

3 Annual usage and value are the two criteria that are most commonly used to classify the importance of inventory.
Other criteria that could be used include: (a) uncertainty of supply; and (b) risk of obsolescence.

An individual item of inventory could be classified as A/A/B - high usage, high value, and medium in terms of risk of obsolescence.

4 There are various ways in which inventory can be measured.
Monetary values can be used to measure the absolute level of inventory at a point in time. This is a useful measure of investment.

Alternative methods involve comparing investment and throughput. There are two basic ways in which this can be done:

- Cover - calculate how long the inventory in the system would last if demand were normal and no replenishment orders were placed.

- Stock turns - calculate how often stock is used up in a given period.

These two measures are actually the reciprocals of each other.

5 Operations need information processing systems to help them manage their inventory.
Inventory management involves large numbers of routine calculations. It is ideally suited for computer applications.

Typical capabilities that might be required include: (a) updating stock records; (b) generating orders; (c) forecasting; and (d) generating inventory reports.

Inventory classifications and measures

Class A items - the 20% or so of high-value items which account for around 80% of the total stock value

Class B items - the next 30% or so of medium-value items which account for around 10% of the total stock value

Class C items - the remaining 50% or so of low-value items which account for around the last 10% of the total stock value

CHAPTER 13

SUPPLY CHAIN PLANNING AND CONTROL

Key questions
• What is the difference between such terms as purchasing, physical distribution, logistics, materials management and supply chain management?
• What is the purpose and objective of purchasing management?
• What is the purpose and objective of physical distribution management?
• How is the concept of supply chain management different?

Topics covered
• Definitions of purchasing, physical distribution management, logistics, materials management and supply chain management.
• Purchasing and supplier development.
• Physical distribution management.
• Integration of the organization's functions through logistics and materials management.
• Integration of organizations through supply chain management.

Summary
What is the difference between such terms as purchasing, physical distribution, logistics, materials management and supply chain management?
• Purchasing is concerned with the supply-side activities of an organization.
• Physical distribution management is the management of the (often multi-echelon) inventory and transportation systems which link the operation with its customers.
• Logistics includes the demand side physical distribution of goods often beyond the immediate customers, through the supply chain to the end customer.
• Materials management is an integrated concept which includes both purchasing activities as well as physical distribution activities.
• Supply chain management is a broader concept which includes the management of the entire supply chain from supplier of raw material to the end customer.

What is the purpose and objective of purchasing management?
• Purchasing includes the formal preparation of requests to suppliers for a quotation, the evaluation of suppliers, the issuing of formal purchase orders, and the monitoring of delivery.
• The purchasing function attempts to obtain goods or services at the right price, for delivery at the right time, with the right quality, in the right quantity, from the right source.
• The effect of savings on the bought-in materials bill in most organizations has a disproportionate effect on profitability. The greater the proportion of their costs which are devoted to bought-in materials, the greater the saving for a given reduction in bought-in material costs.

What is the purpose and objective of physical distribution management?
• Physical distribution management decisions include the number and position of warehouses in the system and the mode of physical transport which needs to be adopted.
• This area also includes the decision as to which contract terms buyers and suppliers agree. The choice of contract defines the responsibility and risk relating to who pays for transportation. There are internationally recognized terms which define the balance of risks and costs. These include such terms as ex-works, free alongside, free on board, cost and freight, cost insurance and freight and delivered.

How is the concept of supply chain management different?

• Supply chain management is a more strategic concept which includes the strategic and long-term consideration of supply management issues as well as the shorter term control of flow through the supply chain.

• The term includes developing an understanding of the dynamic effects (sometimes called the Forrester effect) which governs the amplification of demand changes as they affect upstream operations within the supply chain.

• Supply chain management also includes developing appropriate relationships between individual links within the supply chain. These relationship types (which range from integrated hierarchies through to short-term trading commitments) imply different exchange relationships between suppliers and customers.

Definitions of purchasing and related concepts

Points to make

1 **Operations have networks of suppliers.**
A supply chain is a strand in the supply network along which a set of goods or services flows.

2 **Purchasing or supply management is the function which manages the operation's interface with its suppliers.**

3 **Physical distribution management is the function that manages the operation's interface with its customers.**

4 **Logistics is an extension of physical distribution management.**
Logistics is concerned with the management of information and materials flow from the business.

Logistics is described as an extension of physical distribution management because it considers the operation's end customers as well as its immediate customers.

5 **Materials management is concerned with the management of the flow of materials and information through the operation's immediate supply chain.**
Materials management includes activities such as:

- purchasing;

- inventory management;

- stores management;

- operations planning and control;

- physical distribution management.

6 **Supply chain management is a far broader concept.**
Supply chain management is an holistic approach to managing across organizational boundaries.

Supply chain management is important because it can be strategically advantageous for all the operations in a given supply chain to work together to ensure that the end customer is satisfied.

7 **Organizational integration increases as the emphasis switches from 'purchasing' to 'supply chain management'.**

Managing the supply chain

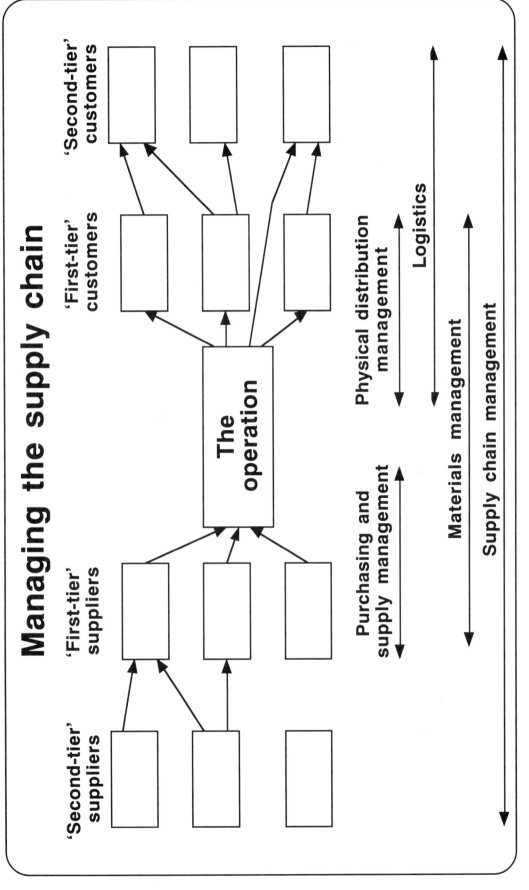

'Second-tier' suppliers

'First-tier' suppliers

'First-tier' customers

'Second-tier' customers

The operation

Purchasing and supply management

Physical distribution management

Logistics

Materials management

Supply chain management

OHP72

Purchasing and supplier development

Points to make

1 Purchasing is responsible for agreeing contracts with suppliers.
The contract specifies the transforming and transformed resources the supplier is to provide.

2 Purchasing is the link between the operation and its suppliers.
For purchasing to be effective it has to understand the requirements of the operation's processes and the capabilities of the operation's suppliers.

3 The purchasing activity can be described as a process.
The purchasing activity involves:
• Operations requesting a product or service.

• Purchasing formally asking potential suppliers to submit quotations which specify how much they would charge if they were asked to provide the product or service.

• Purchasing reviewing the quotations and identifying a preferred supplier.

• Purchasing preparing the necessary purchase agreements - the legal contract. The operations function often needs to be involved in this stage of the process.

• Purchasing closing the loop - checking that the products or services arrive on time and that they are in a satisfactory condition when they arrive.

4 The objectives of purchasing.
Most operations buy in a wide variety of goods and services and in many operations the amount being bought in is increasing.

Goods and services have to be bought in:
• At the right price - purchasing can have a major impact on profitability. Purchasing staff are usually skilled negotiators.

• At the right time and in the right quantity - delivery speed, delivery reliability and flexibility can be reduced if too few goods come in or if the right number of goods arrives too late.

• At the right quality - traditionally goods and services were inspected after delivery. Increasingly suppliers are inspecting their own goods and services prior to dispatch.

• From the right source - the right source is not necessarily the one that can offer the best short-term deal in terms of price, quality and delivery. Other factors, including the rate at which the supplier is improving, need to be considered.

Whenever potential sources of supply are being discussed a key issue is whether the operation should look for single or multiple sources.

5 An essential purchasing decision is the make-buy decision.
The make-buy decision is often based on cost. If the item under consideration can be made cheaper in-house, it will be made in-house. If it cannot, it will be sub-contracted.

The make-buy decision should not be based solely on cost. Other issues to be considered include whether a particular product or service is core, i.e. whether it provides competitive advantage?

Chapter 13

The purchasing process

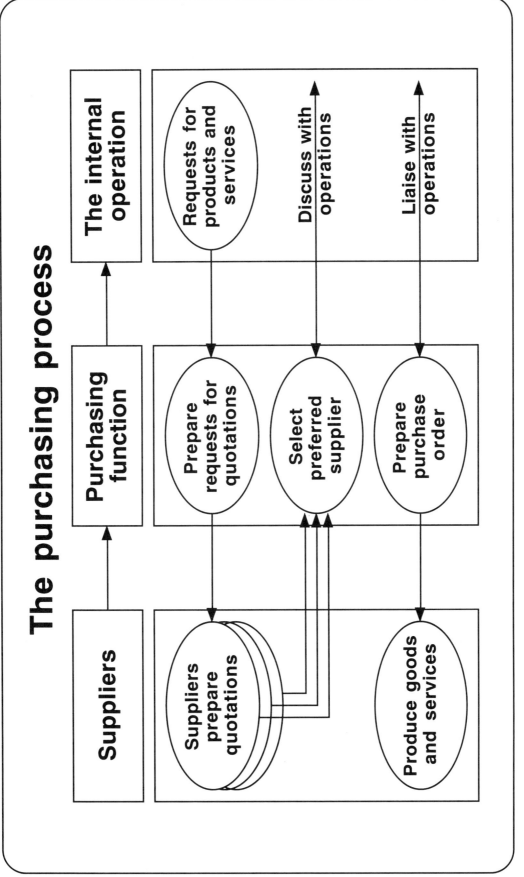

Suppliers

Purchasing function

The internal operation

Suppliers prepare quotations

Prepare requests for quotations

Requests for products and services

Select preferred supplier

Discuss with operations

Prepare purchase order

Liaise with operations

Produce goods and services

OHP73

Physical distribution management

Points to make

1 Goods and services have to be distributed.
On the demand side of the operation the goods and services produced have to be physically distributed. This can be complex, especially in multi-echelon systems. An operation with three factories and six customers has to 'manage' eighteen distribution channels, for example.

2 Warehouses are often used to eliminate some of the problems of physical distribution management.
If factories supply warehouses and customers request goods or services from warehouses, the number of distribution channels that have to be managed is reduced.

3 There are various modes of transport that can be used to distribute goods and services.
Options include road, rail, water, air or even pipelines.

4 The different modes of transport have different characteristics and these affect their suitability for different operations.
The decision as to which mode of transport to use will be influenced by issues such as: (a) delivery speed; (b) delivery reliability; (c) product deterioration; and (d) transportation costs.

5 The mode of transport chosen has implications for the operation.
The mode of transport will affect, or will be affected by, the operation's location. It will also determine the size of the batches that can be transported.

6 The contract agreed between the supplier and customer needs to specify who will be responsible for what.
There are various classes of contract. The most common are:
- Ex-works contracts - the purchaser is responsible for all the costs of transporting the goods from the supplier's location. These costs would include transportation, insurance, documentation, loading and customs.

- Free alongside (FAS) - the supplier is responsible for the costs associated with transporting and insuring the goods until they reach a specified port. The customer is responsible for all the costs thereafter (loading and unloading, insurance, customs).

- Free on board (FOB) - the supplier pays for everything up to, and including, loading on to the outbound transportation. The customer is responsible thereafter.

- Cost and freight (C&F) - the supplier pays for transportation to an agreed place. The customer is responsible for the costs of customs documentation, insurance once the goods have been loaded, and all costs once the goods have been unloaded.

- Cost, insurance and freight (CIF) - this is exactly the same as cost and freight except that the supplier pays for the insurance.

- Delivered - the supplier is responsible for all costs.

7 International distribution is costly and can be risky.
In the 'international pipeline' accidents, piracy, and the fact that inventory is idle for long periods are issues that need to be considered.

Physical distribution management

Operations performance dimension	Mode of transport				
	Road	Rail	Air	Water	Pipeline
Delivery speed	2	3	1	5	4
Reliability	2	3	4	5	1
Quality	2	3	4	5	1
Cost	3	4	5	2	1
Route flexibility	1	2	3	4	5

1 - best performance, 5 - worst performance

Integration of the organization's function

Points to make

1 Both material and information flow through the supply chain.

Information, in the form of orders, flows from the purchaser to the supplier.

Materials, in the form of goods or services, flow from the supplier to the purchaser.

2 There are various ways in which these flows of information and materials can be managed.

Options include: (a) materials management; (b) merchandising; (c) logistics; and (d) supply chain management.

3 The concept of materials management originated in the 1970s.

The rationale underpinning materials management is that costs should be reduced if the flow of materials can be integrated.

Integrated, in this context, means a single function has responsibility for purchasing, expediting, inventory management, stores management, physical distribution management, and product planning and control.

The reason that costs should be reduced is that if a single function owns all of the above activities that function should be able to co-ordinate them, thereby eliminating local optimization.

4 Merchandising is usually associated with retail operations.

Merchandising involves combining the purchasing activity with sales and physical distribution management.

Key technologies in merchandising are bar-coding and electronic point-of-sale systems.

5 Logistics is the co-ordinated movement of materials, information and finished products.

6 Supply chain management involves managing the entire supply chain.

The end customer is the only customer with any 'real' money. Everyone else in the supply chain simply shares this money. Hence the rationale underpinning supply chain management is that everyone in a given supply chain should:
• focus on satisfying the end customer;

• identify and implement strategies aimed at capturing and retaining end-customer business.

There are, however, some barriers to supply chain management:
• The businesses in a given supply chain are usually owned by different people and this makes it difficult to co-ordinate activity.

• Supply chains usually branch. A given supply chain can serve different markets with different needs which require different, and potentially conflicting, strategies.

7 Dynamics exist in supply chains - the Forrester Effect.

Volatility in supply chains exists because of supply chain dynamics and time lags.

Integrating the organization's functions

- Options for integrating the organization's functions:

  - materials management;

  - merchandising;

  - logistics;

  - supply chain management.

Integration through supply chain management

Points to make

1   A key question every organization has to address is how much of the supply chain should it seek to own?

2   Ownership is not the only method of supply chain integration.
In fact the options vary from 'integrated hierarchy' through to 'short-term trading commitment'.

3   Integrated hierarchy is the term used to describe a fully vertically integrated firm.
A fully vertically integrated firm is one that houses all activities, from raw material sourcing through to dispatch to the end customer, on a single site.

The major advantage of a fully vertically integrated firm is that it has no need to manage the exchange of information, orders or materials with outside agencies.

4   Semi-hierarchies exist when the firms in a given supply chain are owned by the same group.
The advantages of semi-hierarchies are that they can: (a) centralize purchasing which can lead to volume discounts; (b) operate common systems and technologies; and (c) easily transfer people, materials and even money.

5   Co-contracting involves long-term alliances rather than mergers.
Usually long-term alliances are based on a transfer of equity, as well as people, technologies, goods and services.

Co-contracting, which includes partnerships, can reduce an individual operation's freedom of action, but at least allows the individual operations to retain their own legal identities, cultures and strategies.

6   Co-ordinated-contracting involves prime contractors who employ sub-contractors.
Co-ordinated-contracting is usually carried out on a job-by-job basis. The prime contractors will win the business and employ the sub-contractors who provide their own tools and equipment.

The formal relationship between the prime contractor and sub-contractors terminates at the end of the job.

7   Co-ordinated revenue links are used in licensing or franchising.
Co-ordinated revenue links transfer ownership of a given operation but guarantees income for the licensor or franchiser.

8   Medium- to long-term trading commitments are established when businesses agree to trade with each other for extended periods without formal contracts.

9   Short-term trading commitments are entered into on a transaction-by-transaction basis.
Short-term trading commitments usually involve a competitive tendering process. One problem with this is that it does not necessarily lead to the lowest life cycle cost.

Increasing degrees of integration

Fully vertically integrated

Semi-hierarchy

Co-contracting

Co-ordinated contracting

Co-ordinated revenue links

Medium- to long-term trading commitments

Short-term trading commitments

OHP76

CHAPTER 14

MRP

Key questions
• What is MRP ?
• What is the process involved in MRP planning and control?
• What are the main elements in an MRP system?
• What is 'closed loop' MRP?
• What is MRP II?

Topics covered
• The meaning of MRP - both MRP and MRP.
• What is required to run MRP.
• The process of MRP
• Closed-loop MRP.
• The concept of MRP.

Summary

What is MRP ?
• MRP stands for Materials Requirements Planning which is a dependent demand system which calculates materials requirements and production plans to satisfy known and forecast sales orders.
• MRP helps make volume and timing calculations based on an idea of what will be necessary to supply demand in the future.

What is the process involved in MRP planning and control?
• MRP works from a master production schedule which summarizes the volume and timing of end products or services.
• The master production schedule is a slightly more detailed version of the aggregated capacity plans which were discussed in Chapter 11.
• Using the logic of the product or services bill of materials (BOM) and the inventory records of the operation the production schedule is 'exploded' to determine how many sub-assemblies and parts are required and when they are required to achieve the master production schedule.
• This process of exploding the master production schedule is called the MRP netting process. It is carried out throughout the different levels of the product structure.
• Within this process 'back-scheduling' takes into account the lead-time required to obtain parts at each level of the assembly.

What are the main elements in an MRP system?
• A demand management system must interface with customers in order to set the requirements for the master production schedule.
• The master production schedule is the central reference source for what the system is supposed to produce and when.
• Bills of materials and product structure information together with lead times, enable the netting process to take place.
• Inventory records contain data which allows the MRP system to understand where stock is located, how many parts are in stock and what issue and receipt transactions have occurred against any parts.
• The output from the materials requirement planning system are purchase orders, materials plans and works orders which trigger the purchasing or manufacture of parts.

What is 'closed loop' MRP?

• Closed-loop MRP systems contain feedback loops which ensure that checks are made against capacity to see if plans are feasible.

What is MRP II?

• MRP II systems are a development of MRP which integrate many processes which are related to MRP, but located outside the operations function.

• Without MRP II separate databases would be held for different functions.

• A system which performs roughly the same function as MRP II is Optimized Production Technology (OPT). It is based on the theory of constraints which has been developed to focus attention on capacity bottlenecks in the operation.

The meaning of MRP

Points to make

1 **MRP systems were designed to help businesses plan and control their resource requirements.**
MRP systems are computer-based information processing systems.

2 **The concept of MRP has developed over time.**
Originally MRP systems were designed to help the operations function plan and control its resource requirements.

Now they are designed to help the business plan and control its resource requirements.

3 **MRP used to mean material requirements planning.**
The first MRP systems came on line in the 1960s.

These early MRP systems enabled companies:

- to calculate how much material of particular types were required;

- to calculate when it was required;

- to check whether the necessary components would be available at the right time;

- to raise works and purchase orders for any components that would not be available at the right time so that they could be made available.

4 **Material requirements planning basically involves a series of simple, but interrelated, decisions about the quantity and timing of materials.**
The materials requirements planning process is ideally suited to computer application.

5 **The material requirements planning concept can be expanded to other parts of the business.**
Manufacturing resource planning (MRP2) enables companies to examine the engineering and financial impact of future demand, as well as the material requirements.

The meaning of MRP

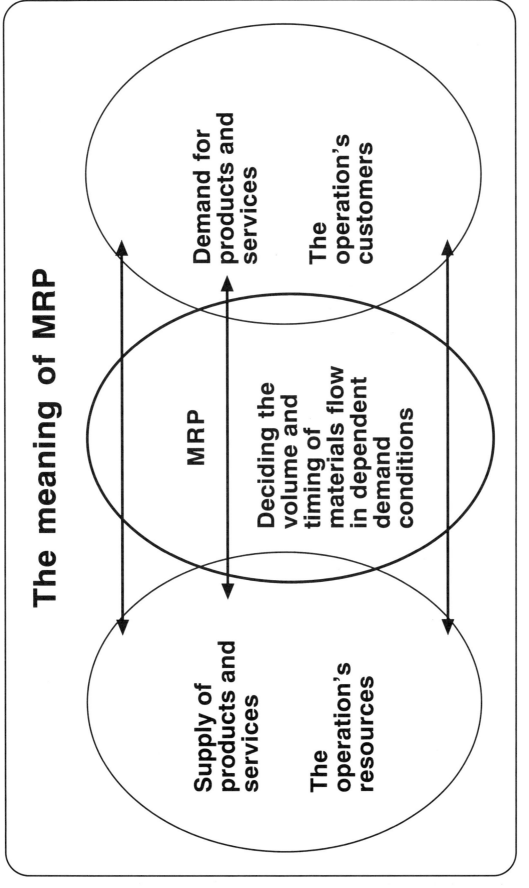

Demand for products and services

The operation's customers

MRP

Deciding the volume and timing of materials flow in dependent demand conditions

Supply of products and services

The operation's resources

OHP77

What is required to run MRP1?

Points to make

1   As MRP is a computer-based information processing system various computer files, each of which must be kept up to date, are required to run it.

2   **The inputs to the MRP include firm customer orders and forecast demand.**

Firm orders are those that have been confirmed. They can be specified in terms of quantity and due date. It must always be remembered that customers may change their minds.

Forecast orders are those that the organization can reasonably expect to receive, but which it has not received to date. Accurate forecasting is extremely difficult. The credibility of a forecast decreases as its time horizon increases.

All the calculations performed during the MRP process are dependent upon these two sets of data. Hence the accuracy of these data will have a major impact on the effectiveness of the MRP system.

3   **The master production schedule (MPS) is the most important planning and control schedule in the business.**

The master production schedule (MPS): (a) summarizes what the business plans to make; (b) drives the whole operation in terms of what is assembled, what is made and what is bought in; (c) forms the basis of planning the utilization of labour and equipment; and (d) determines the provision of materials and cash.

The master production schedule is calculated by looking at future demand, assessing what inventory is available and then entering on to the MPS the details of any orders that cannot be met from the available inventory.

For this planning process to work it is vital that the operation keeps track of what will be 'available to promise' in any given week.

4   **The bill of materials provides a record of the components that go into each product.**

The bill of materials specifies which parts go into which products in what quantity.

To simplify their complexity, bills of materials are structured around levels. Level 0 is the finished product. Level 1 describes the sub-assemblies that go into this finished product. Level 2 describes the components that go into the sub-assemblies, and so on. The bill of materials, for a given operation, stops when the part being described in it is not made by the business.

5   **Accurate inventory records are fundamental to MRP1.**

MRP1 requires inventory records which describe:

- each item of stock (part number, part description, supplier, unit cost, lead time for supply) - this information is stored in the item master file;

- the location of each item of stock - his information is stored in the location file;

- any transactions regarding each item of stock - this information is stored in the transaction file.

What is required to run MRP1?

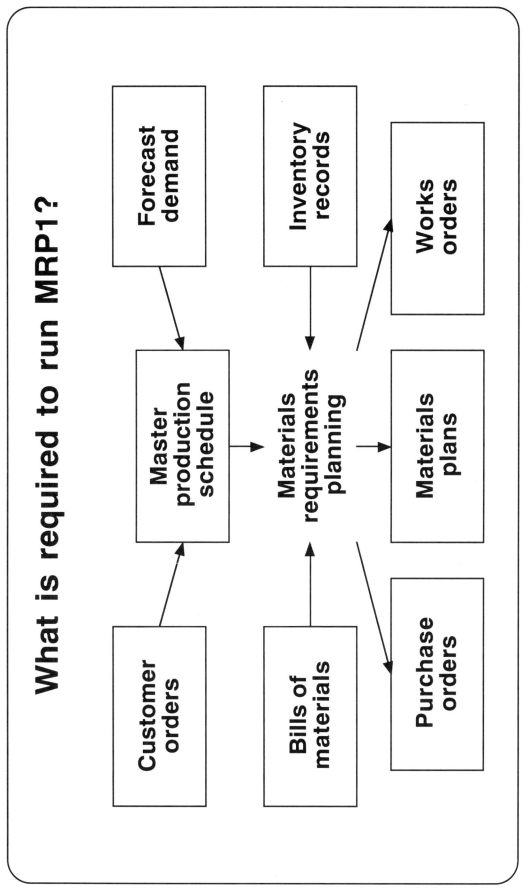

The process of MRP1

Points to make

1 MRP1 is a systematic process.

MRP1 takes planning information and uses it to calculate the volume and timing requirements that will satisfy demand.

2 The MRP netting process 'explodes' the MPS.

The MRP netting process uses the first level of the bill of materials to calculate how many sub-assemblies and parts have to be available at specific times if the MPS is to be achieved.

Before moving on to the next level, the MRP system checks how many of these parts are in stock and free to promise.

The MRP system then generates works and purchase orders for any parts that are not available, and then moves on to repeat the process at the next level of the bill of materials.

Through this process the MRP system calculates what assemblies, sub-assemblies, parts and materials need to be made or bought in for the MPS to be achieved.

3 The MRP backscheduling process takes account of the fact that parts and assemblies cannot be made available instantaneously.

Every item that is required has a lead time associated with it. Parts that are bought in from outside have to be ordered and delivered. Parts that are made in-house have to be manufactured.

Backscheduling is the process MRP uses to identify when activities have to begin for the MPS to be achieved.

The MRP item master file contains data on the lead time for each item. Every works and purchase order the MRP system generates, identifies the date at which manufacturing has to begin, or the order has to be placed, if the item is to be available by its required due date.

4 The MRP process is further complicated by batching rules.

Works and purchase orders cannot always be released for the exact number of items required. Most operations have batching rules which specify how many units should be produced, for reasons of machine utilization, or how many items should be ordered (the economic order quantity).

The MRP process has to take account of these batching rules.

The process of MRP1

- Explode the master production schedule.

- Identify what parts and assemblies are required.

- Check whether the required parts and assemblies are available.

- For every part or assembly that is required, but not available, identify when work needs to be started for it to be made available by its due date.

- Generate the appropriate works and purchase orders.

- Repeat the process for the next level of the bill of materials.

Closed-loop MRP

Points to make

1   MRP was originally designed as an operations planning tool.
The materials plans were released at the start of each week and the MRP system was run again at the end of the week to generate the following week's plan.

When MRP was operating in this mode no attempt was made to assess whether:

• the plan for a given week was achievable;

• the plan for the previous week had been achieved.

2   Closed-loop MRP uses feedback to do this.

3   Closing the loop involves checking production plans against resource availability.
MRP1 effectively assumes that the operation has infinite resources. Closed-loop MRP checks whether sufficient resources are available to meet the proposed production plan. If sufficient resources are not available the plan is modified.

4   There are three basic planning routines in closed-loop MRP.
Resource requirements planning:

• This involves long-term strategic plans.

• It looks at whether the operation is likely to have sufficient capacity to meet demand in the long term, and if not whether new plants should be built, or existing plants expanded.

Rough-cut capacity planning:

• This is a medium- to short-term finite capacity plan.

• It involves assessing whether the operation has sufficient capacity to achieve the medium- to short-term production plans.

• Normally the analysis is based around known bottlenecks and other key resources, on the grounds that if they have sufficient capacity then the rest of the operation should be safe.

Capacity requirements planning:

• This is a short-term capacity plan.

• It involves looking at the load profile for the organization's resources and assessing whether work should be rescheduled so that peaks and troughs in demand can be smoothed out.

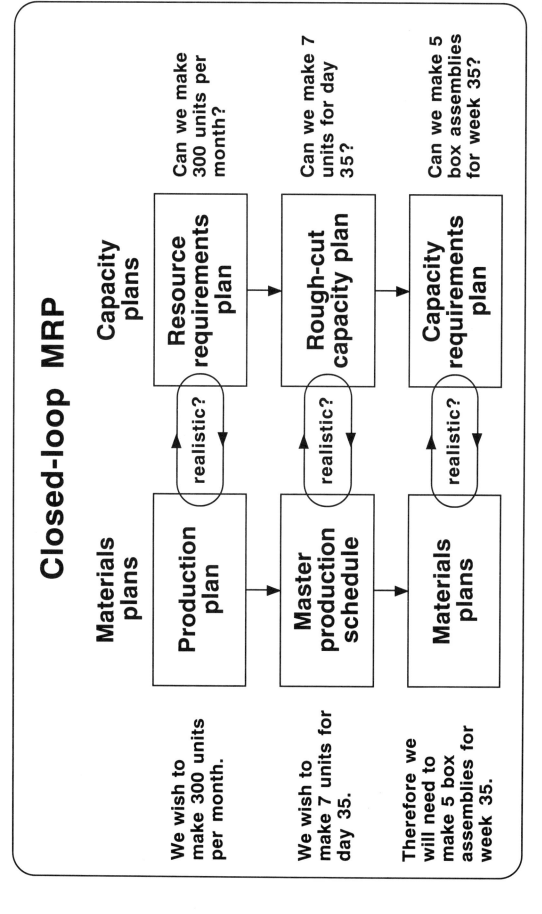

OHP80

The concept of MRP2

Points to make

1   MRP2 extends the concept of MRP1.

MRP2 seeks to apply the principles of MRP1 to other areas of the business.

Essentially MRP2 involves using closed-loop MRP to assess the financial implications of the materials requirements plans.

2   MRP2 relies on a single integrated database.

Organizations which do not operate MRP2 systems tend to hold duplicate sets of information on different databases.

One of the major advantages of MRP2 is that it relies on a single integrated database which reduces the chances of the operation holding conflicting pieces of data in different locations.

3   Other materials planning and control packages are available. One such package is optimized production technology (OPT).

OPT consists of two things:

- some software - used for scheduling;

- some 'thoughtware' - the ten rules of OPT.

OPT's focus is on bottlenecks. It seeks to maximize bottleneck utilization on the grounds that the bottlenecks control the operation's output.

4   MRP and OPT do not conflict.

MRP and OPT can be used simultaneously. They rely on the same data, with one major exception. MRP assumes that lead times are fixed, whereas OPT argues that they are a function of the schedule.

The concept of MRP2

```
   ┌──────────┐                      ┌──────────┐
   │ Marketing│                      │  Finance │
   └────┬─────┘                      └────┬─────┘
        │                                 │
        └──────────┐          ┌───────────┘
                   ▼          ▼
              ╭─────────────────╮
              │                 │
              │     Central     │
              │    database     │
              │                 │
              ╰─────────────────╯
                   ▲          ▲
        ┌──────────┘          └───────────┐
        │                                 │
   ┌────┴─────┐                      ┌────┴─────┐
   │  Design  │                      │Operations│
   └──────────┘                      └──────────┘
```

CHAPTER 15

JUST-IN-TIME PLANNING AND CONTROL

Key questions
- What is JIT and how is it different from traditional operations practice?
- What are the main elements of JIT philosophy?
- What are the techniques of JIT?
- How can JIT be used for planning and control?
- Can JIT be used in service operations?
- Can JIT and MRP co-exist?

Topics covered
- The meaning of JIT and how it differs from more traditional operations practice.
- The overall philosophy of JIT and its origins in Japanese manufacturing and culture.
- The range of techniques which are commonly associated with JIT operations.
- The specific planning and control techniques of JIT.
- How JIT and MRP approaches can co-exist and how operations can choose between them.

Summary
What is JIT and how is it different from traditional operations practice?
- JIT (just-in-time) is an approach to operations which tries to meet demand instantaneously with perfect quality and no waste.
- It is an approach which differs from traditional operations practices in so much as it stresses waste elimination and fast throughput, both of which contribute to low inventories.
- The ability to deliver just-in-time not only saves working capital (through reducing inventory levels) but also has a significant impact on the ability of an operation to improve its intrinsic efficiency.

What are the main elements of JIT philosophy?
- As a philosophy, JIT can be summarized as three overlapping elements. These are,
    - the elimination of waste in the operation. This is best visualized as the time wasted as materials, information or customers move through the system.
    - the inclusion of all staff of the operation in its improvement. In this way it is similar to some of the ideas described in Chapter 9
    - the idea that all improvement should be on a continuous basis. This is explored in greater depth in Chapter 18.
- A common feature of JIT philosophy is the progressive removal of (surplus) resources so as to enable the operation to learn how to manage without these resources.

What are the techniques of JIT?

• The techniques which are usually associated with JIT (not specifically concerned with planning and control, see next point) are
- developing 'basic working practices' which support waste elimination and continuous improvement.
- design for manufacture.
- focused operations which reduce complexity.
- using simple,small machines which are robust and flexible.
- rearranging layout and flow to enhance simplicity of flow.
- employing total productive maintenance (see Chapter 19) to encourage reliability.
- reducing set-up time and changeover times to enhance flexibility.
- involving all staff in the improvement of the operation.
- making any problems visible to all staff.
- extending the above principles to suppliers

How can JIT be used for planning and control?

• Many JIT techniques directly concern planning and control. They are:
- Pull scheduling
- Kanban control
- Levelled scheduling
- Mixed model scheduling
- Synchronization of flow

Can JIT be used in service operations?

• Many of the above techniques are directly applicable in service operations although some translation occasionally is required.

Can JIT and MRP coexist?

• Although JIT and MRP might be seen to be very different approaches to planning and control, they can be combined to form a hybrid system.

• The way in which JIT and MRP can be combined depends on the complexity of product structures and of product routing, the volume-variety characteristics of the operation and the level of control required.

The meaning of just-in-time

Points to make

1   Literally JIT means producing goods and services exactly when they are needed - not too early, not too late.
Quality and efficiency targets often accompany this time-based requirement.

2   JIT is a philosophy - a way of working.
By adopting JIT an operation will not suddenly be able to deliver exactly what is wanted, exactly when it is wanted. Instead it will have started on a journey which might ultimately enable it to achieve this goal.

3   JIT is different to traditional methods of planning and control.
Traditional production control systems guarantee the independence of resources through inventory buffers which provide protection from disruptions. The rationale underlying the traditional approach is that even if part of the operation is disrupted, the rest of it should be able to keep running because of the inventory buffers. As a result traditional production control systems lead to high resource utilization, high levels of work in progress and long throughput times.

JIT seeks to eliminate inventory on the grounds that it hides an operation's intrinsic inefficiencies. If inventory is removed, disruptions will have a major impact and hence the root causes of the disruptions are likely to be sought and eliminated.

4   JIT requires improvement in all the performance objectives.
Quality. When operating a JIT system any disruption will have a major impact, hence quality problems have to be eliminated.

Speed. In a JIT environment little work in progress is held. Production effectively occurs on a make-to-order basis, hence fast throughput is essential.

Dependability. A prerequisite to fast throughput.

Flexibility. One way of achieving fast throughput is to keep the batch size small. Flexibility is a prerequisite if batch sizes are to be kept small.

5   JIT requires some sacrifice of capacity utilization.
Achieving high standards of performance in all of the objectives requires some sacrifice. In JIT's case it is reduced capacity utilization.

It should be noted, however, that high levels of utilization do not always lead to increased output. In fact, high levels of utilization can simply result in increased stock.

The meaning of just-in-time

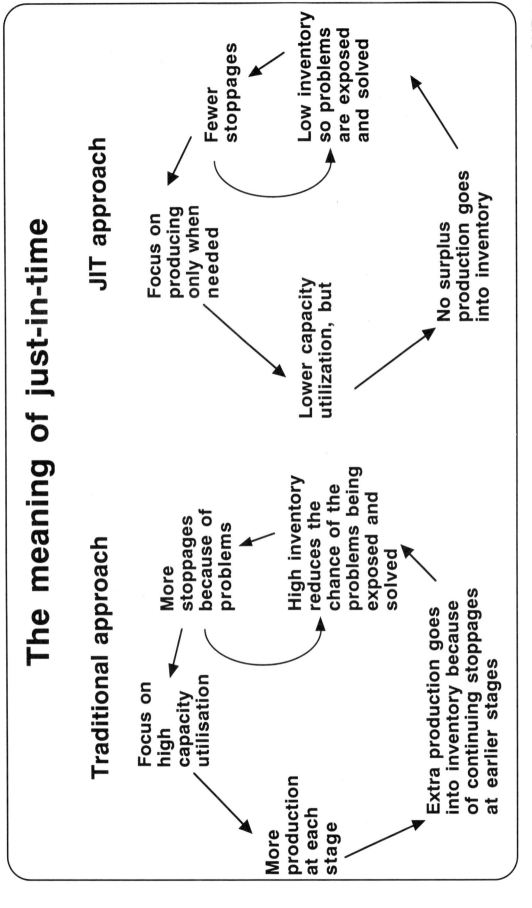

Traditional approach

Focus on high capacity utilisation

More production at each stage

More stoppages because of problems

High inventory reduces the chance of the problems being exposed and solved

Extra production goes into inventory because of continuing stoppages at earlier stages

JIT approach

Focus on producing only when needed

Fewer stoppages

Low inventory so problems are exposed and solved

Lower capacity utilization, but

No surplus production goes into inventory

The JIT philosophy and its origins

Points to make

1   If JIT is to be understood it has to be viewed at two levels.
JIT is a philosophy which can be used to guide the actions of operations managers.

JIT is a set of tools and techniques.

2   The JIT philosophy basically involves doing simple things well.
And gradually doing them better - squeezing out waste.

3   Culture played a large part in the development of JIT.
JIT was developed in Japan - a crowded country with few natural resources and a tendency to 'make every grain of rice count'.

Given their environment, it is not surprising that the Japanese were receptive to JIT - a high dependency philosophy which emphasizes low waste and high value added.

4   JIT has three key elements.
The elimination of waste:

- Waste is defined as any activity that does not add value.

- Toyota identified seven categories of waste: overproduction, waiting time, processes which only exist because of poor product design, transport, inventory, motion and defective goods.

Total employee involvement:

- The JIT philosophy respects the contribution humans can make.

- It encourages a high degree of personal responsibility, engagement and ownership, through team-based problem solving, job enrichment, job rotation and multi-skilling.

Continuous improvement:

- The objectives of JIT (zero waste, zero inventory, etc.) are ideals from which the operations' current levels of performance may be far removed.

- Central to JIT is the notion of continuous improvement - continuously striving to identify ways in which things can be done better.

The JIT philosophy

JIT as a philosophy

- Eliminate waste
- Involve everyone
- Continuous improvement

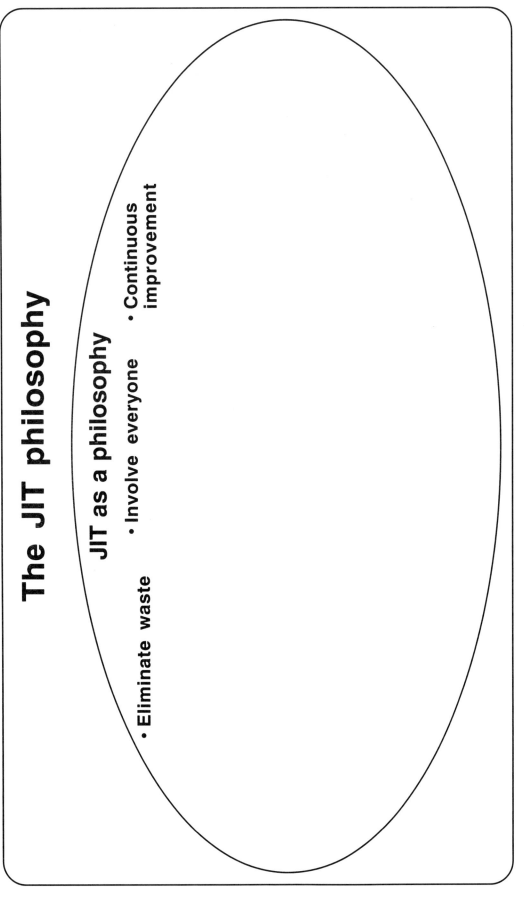

The range of techniques commonly associated with JIT

Points to make

1   The 'engine room' of JIT is a set of tools and techniques aimed at eliminating waste.

2   The operation's basic working practices are important.
To operate effectively JIT requires: (a) equality; (b) discipline; (c) flexibility; (d) autonomy; (e) personnel development; and (f) creativity.

Quality of working life also needs to be considered. JIT operations often: (a) involve people in decision making; (b) offer people security of employment; (c) try to design jobs so that they are enjoyable; and (d) make sure that each area's working facilities are appropriate.

3   Design for manufacture is an approach associated with JIT.
Design for manufacture can result in substantial cost savings.

4   JIT operations take an operational focus on the grounds that simplicity, repetition and experience breed competence.

5   Small, simple machines are common in organizations using JIT.
JIT operations often buy in basic technologies and then modify them to meet the organization's needs. This reduces risk, makes it easier to maintain the equipment and improves in-house engineering skills.

6   The layout of JIT operations is considered carefully.
Most JIT lines are kept simple. Cells, often laid out in 'U' shapes, are common. Workstations are kept close together and the whole operation is kept transparent.

7   Total productive maintenance is used to eliminate unplanned breakdowns.
Total productive maintenance (TPM) encourages 'process owners' to do their own maintenance whenever possible and to call on skilled engineers only when they are really needed. This not only enhances the process owner's job, but also frees up the engineers to tackle higher order problems.

8   Set-up reduction is fundamental in JIT operations.
Set-up reduction is achieved by identifying which set-up activities can be done while the machine is still running. Improvements often include presetting tools, standardizing jigs and fixtures, and simplifying the loading and unloading of tools and dies.

9   JIT operations tend to rely on visibility.
JIT operations are often open plan. Andon lights are used to indicate whether machines are working, idle, or broken. Statistical process control data are displayed, as are samples of good and bad output, and competitor products.

10   Suppliers are heavily involved in the process.
Suppliers to JIT operations are expected to deliver what is wanted, when it is wanted. They are encouraged and helped to implement JIT in their own operations.

Techniques commonly associated with JIT

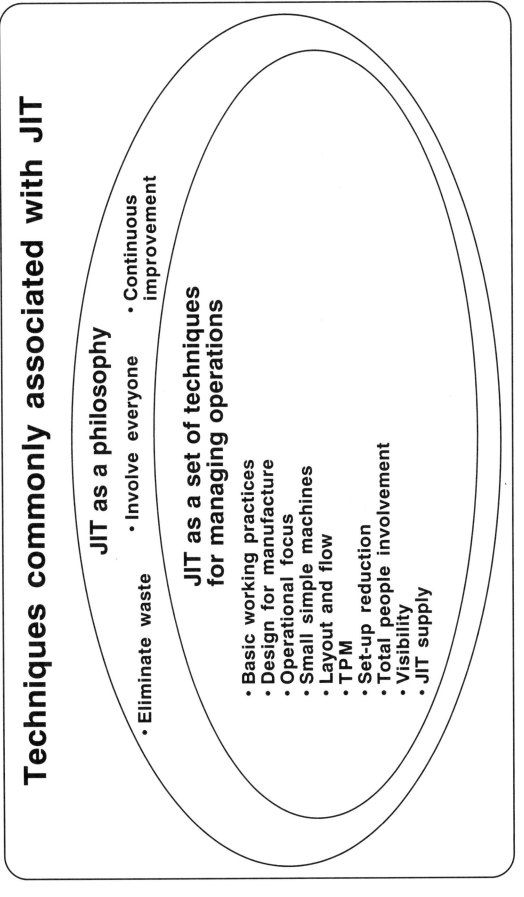

JIT as a philosophy

- Eliminate waste
- Involve everyone
- Continuous improvement

JIT as a set of techniques
for managing operations

- Basic working practices
- Design for manufacture
- Operational focus
- Small simple machines
- Layout and flow
- TPM
- Set-up reduction
- Total people involvement
- Visibility
- JIT supply

OHP84

Specific planning and control techniques of JIT

Points to make

1 JIT planning and control is based on a pull system.

Inventory timing is seen as a source of waste. Hence JIT operations seek to co-ordinate the flow of materials through the operation so that they are available exactly when they are needed.

Four techniques are used to do this: (a) kanban control; (b) levelled scheduling; (c) mixed modelling; and (d) synchronization.

2 The word *kanban* is the Japanese for card or signal.

Kanban cards are effectively invisible conveyors. They control the flow of materials through the operation.

In their simplest form kanban cards are used by customers to instruct their suppliers to start work. Sometimes plastic trays or boxes painted on the floor are used instead of cards.

3 There are three types of kanban.

Conveyance kanbans are used as a signal that material should be withdrawn from a particular store and sent to a particular place.

Production kanbans are used as a signal that a production process can start work.

Vendor kanbans are used as a signal that a supplier should send materials or parts.

4 The fundamental rule is that work can only be started once a kanban has been received.

5 Levelled scheduling seeks to make sure that the mix and volume in the production schedule is constant over time.

In theory, levelled scheduling is simple. In practice, it is extremely difficult, but it can be advantageous because of the regularity and rhythm it provides.

6 Mixed modelling takes levelled scheduling one stage further.

Mixed modelling seeks to design the schedule so that it repeats itself very frequently. In their drive for mixed modelling, some operations have effectively managed to reduce the economic batch quantity to one.

7 Synchronization seeks to pace the production process.

The aim of synchronization is to ensure that the production process follows a regular and predictable drumbeat.

8 A prerequisite to synchronization is part classification.

One of the most common classification systems is:

• runners - parts which are produced frequently;

• repeaters - parts which are produced regularly;

• strangers - parts which are produced irregularly.

JIT planning and control

JIT as a philosophy

- Eliminate waste
- Involve everyone
- Continuous improvement

JIT as a set of techniques for managing operations

- Basic working practices
- Design for manufacture
- Operational focus
- Small simple machines
- Layout and flow
- TPM
- Set-up reduction
- Total people involvement
- Visibility
- JIT supply

JIT as a method of planning and control

- Pull scheduling
- Kanban control
- Levelled scheduling
- Mixed modelling
- Synchronization

How JIT and MRP can co-exist

Points to make

1 Are JIT and MRP fundamentally opposing philosophies?

JIT is a pull-based system of planning and control. It is designed to pull work through the system in response to customer demand.

MRP is a push-based planning and control system. It is designed to push work through the system.

2 JIT and MRP can co-exist because they have different strengths.

3 The aim of MRP is to deliver goods just when needed.

MRP does this by looking forward and asking what has to be produced to meet future demand.

MRP is good at:
• planning future demand;

• tying customer demand to the supplier network;

• coping with complexity.

4 JIT performs best in stable conditions.

JIT performs best when:
• the product structures are relatively simple;

• the material flow is clearly defined;

• demand is level and predictable.

5 How might MRP and JIT be used together?

MRP could be used for strangers and JIT for runners and repeaters.

Alternatively MRP could be used for overall planning and control - to check whether there is enough material in the pipeline. JIT could then be used to call off these materials and for internal control.

This approach has several advantages.
• There is no need for internal interstage works orders.

• In-process inventory need only be monitored between cells rather than for each activity.

• The bill of materials has fewer levels than in a conventional MRP system.

• Process route information is simplified.

• Work centre planning and control is simplified.

• Lead times and work in progress is reduced.

6 When should JIT be used and when should MRP be used?

The answer to this question depends on the operation's complexity, its volume-variety position and the level of control required.

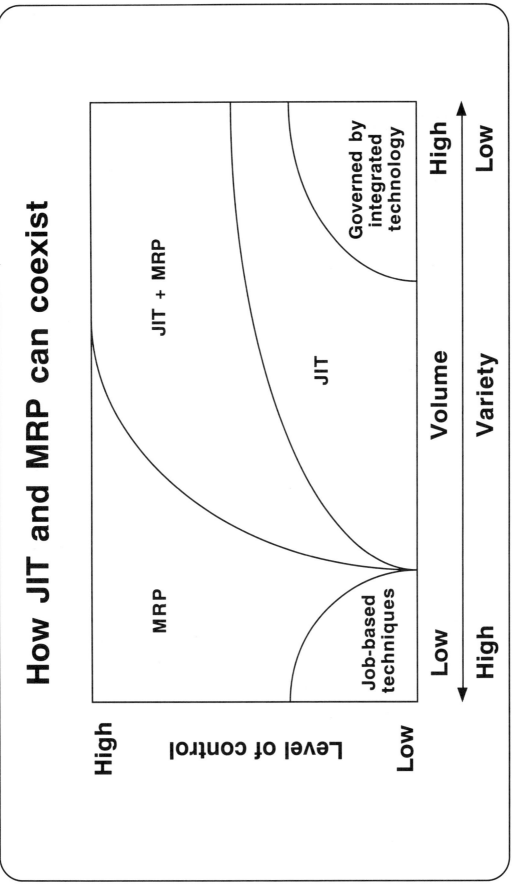

How JIT and MRP can coexist

CHAPTER 16

PROJECT PLANNING AND CONTROL

Key questions
• What is a project and what is project management?
• Why is it important to understand the environment in which a project takes place?
• How are specific projects defined?
• What is project planning and why is it important?
• What techniques can be used for project planning?
• What is project control and how is it done?

Topics covered
• The nature of projects and project management.
• The environment in which projects take place.
• How projects can be defined in terms of their objectives, their scope and the strategy for their completion.
• How projects are planned.
• How projects are controlled.
• How network analysis can be used for planning and controlling projects.

Summary
What is a project and what is project management?
• A project is a set of activities which has a defined start point and a defined end state, that pursues a defined goal and that uses a defined set of resources.
• All projects can be characterized by their degree of complexity and the inherent uncertainty in the project.
• Project management is the process of managing the activities within a project by planning the work, executing it and co-ordinating the contribution of the staff and organizations who have an interest in the project.
• Project management has five stages, four of which are relevant to project planning and control. These are:
  Stage 1 - understanding the project environments
  Stage 2 - defining the project
  Stage 3 - planning the project
  Stage 4 - technical execution of the project (not part of project planning and control)
  Stage 5 - project control.

Why is it important to understand the environment in which a project takes place?
• It is important for two reasons. First, the environment influences the way a project is carried out. Second, the nature of the environment in which a project takes place is the main determinant of the uncertainty surrounding it.

How are specific projects defined?
• Projects can be defined in terms of
  - their objectives - the end state which project management is trying to achieve.
  - their scope - the exact range of responsibilities taken on by project management.
  - their strategy - how project management is going to meet the project objectives.

What is project planning and why is it important?

• Project planning involves five stages:

  Identifying the activities within a project;

  Estimating times and resources for activities;

  Identifying the relationships and dependencies between the activities;

  Identifying the schedule constraints;

  Fixing the schedule.

• Project planning is particularly important where complexity of the project is high. The interrelationship between activities, resources and times in most projects, especially complex ones, is such that unless they are carefully planned, resources can become seriously overloaded at times during the operation.

What techniques can be used for project planning?

• Network planning and Gantt charts are the most common techniques. The former (either using activity-on-arrow or activity-on-node format) is particularly useful for assessing the total duration of a project and the degree of flexibility or float of the individual activities within the project.

• The most common method of network planning is called critical path method (CPM).

• The logic inherent in a network diagram can be changed by resource constraints.

• Network planning models can also be used to assess the total cost of shortening a project where individual activities are shortened .

What is project control and how is it done?

• The process of project control involves three sets of decisions: how to monitor the project to check its progress, how to assess the performance of the project by comparing monitored observations to the project plan, and how to intervene in the project in order to make the changes to bring it back to plan.

• Earned value control assesses the performance of the project by combining cost and time together. It involves plotting the actual expenditure on the project against the value of the work completed, both in the form of what was planned and what is actually happening. Both cost and schedule variances can then be detected.

The nature of projects and project management

Points to make

1   A project is a set of activities which: (a) has a defined start point; (b) has a defined end state; (c) pursues a defined goal; and (d) uses a defined set of resources.

2   To plan and control a project, a model which describes its complexity has to be devised.
By projecting this model forward in time the model can be turned into a plan, which can be used to check progress as the real project proceeds (control of the project).

3   All projects have elements in common.
These are: (a) an objective - definable end result, output or product; (b) complexity - large number of different tasks; (c) uniqueness - projects are usually 'one-offs'; (d) uncertainty - projects are planned before they are executed hence they carry an element of risk; (e) temporary nature - defined beginning and end; and (f) life cycle - resource needs change during the life of the project.

4   Programmes are different to projects.
Programmes have no defined end point.

5   Projects can be categorized according to:
- Their complexity - in terms of size, value and the number of people involved in the project. Complex projects are not necessarily difficult to plan, but they can be difficult to control because of the large number of activities they involve.

- Their uncertainty - in terms of achieving the project objectives of cost, time and quality. Uncertainty makes projects difficult to plan because it makes it difficult to define and set realistic objectives.

Projects which are both complex and have high uncertainty are particularly difficult to manage.

6   Successful project management depends upon various factors:
Some of the key factors are: (a) clearly defined goals; (b) competent project manager; (c) top management support; (d) competent project team members; (e) sufficient resource allocation; (f) adequate communication; (g) control mechanisms; (h) feedback capabilities; (i) responsiveness to clients; (j) trouble-shooting mechanisms; and (k) project staff continuity.

7   Project planning and control consists of five stages:
Stage 1 - understanding the project environment. The internal and external factors which may influence the project.

Stage 2 - defining the project. Setting the objectives, scope and strategy for the project.

Stage 3 - project planning. Deciding how the project will be executed.

Stage 4 - technical execution . Performing the technical aspects of the project.

Stage 5 - project control. Ensuring that the project is carried out according to plan.

These stages are iterative, rather than sequential.

The nature of projects and project management

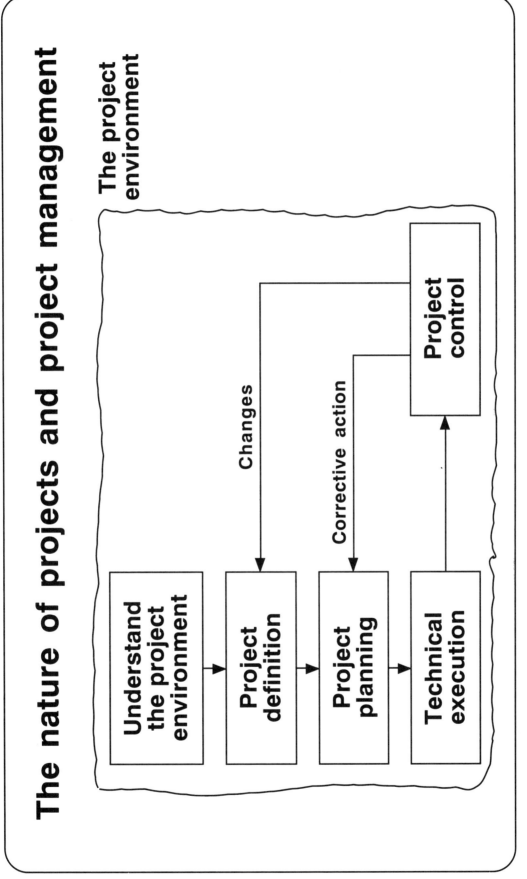

The project environment

Understand the project environment → Project definition → Project planning → Technical execution

Changes

Corrective action

Project control

OHP87

The environment in which projects take place

Points to make

1   Understanding the environment in which the project takes place is important.

Partly because the environment influences the way the project will be executed and also because the environment is the main determinant of the uncertainty inherent in the project.

2   There are a number of dimensions to the project environment.

- Geography - projects in land-locked countries can be subject to serious delays because of shipment problems in neighbouring countries.

- Finance - fluctuating commodity prices and exchange rates.

- Politics - political stance of host government and chance of political dissent.

- Local laws - local labour laws, holiday entitlements and wages.

- National culture - language, customs and expectations.

- Needs of the users - the full needs and expectations of users are not always apparent to outside agencies.

The environment in which projects take place

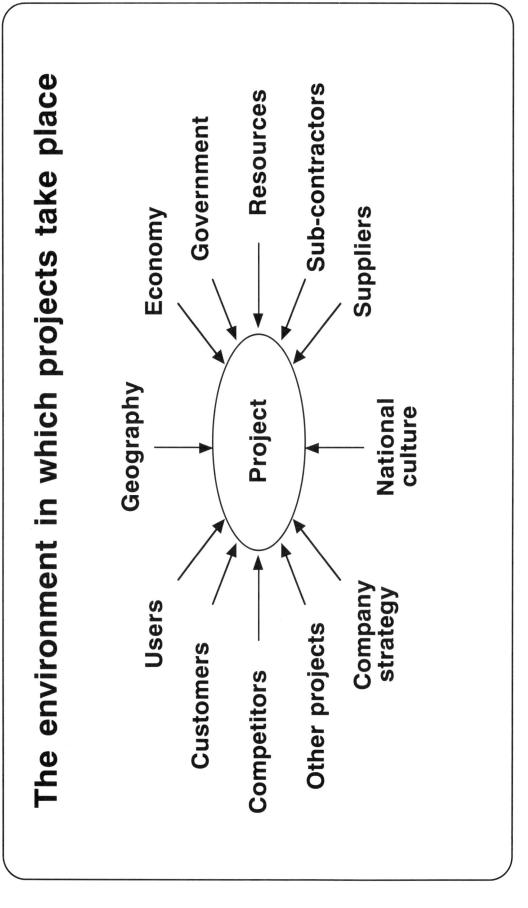

How projects can be defined

Points to make

1 Three different elements are needed to define projects: objectives, scope and strategy.

2 Objectives define the end state project management is trying to achieve.

The objectives: (a) provide overall direction for the project; (b) help staff focus on the rationale of the project and its expected results; and (c) provide a definition of the end point which can be used to monitor progress and to identify when success has been achieved.

3 It is often useful to phrase objectives in user, not designer, terms.

4 Projects have a hierarchy of objectives.

Any project can be disaggregated into a set of sub-projects. Each sub-project has its own objectives, which must be consistent with the overall objectives of the project.

5 Objectives must be clear.

One way of ensuring that the objectives are clear is to break them down into three categories: (a) purpose; (b) end result; and (c) success criteria - defined in terms of quality, cost and time. In project management flexibility is assumed, and speed and dependability are combined into the single category time.

The relative importance of these objectives will vary from project to project.

6 Scope defines the exact range of the responsibilities taken on by project management.

Establishing the scope is really a boundary-setting exercise in that the scope should specify: (a) what the project will do; (b) what the project will not do; and (c) who will be responsible for what.

Defining the project scope involves identifying: (a) the parts of the organization that will be affected by the project; (b) the time period involved; (c) the business processes involved; (d) the resources to be used; and (e) the contractor's responsibilities. It is important that the contractor's responsibilities are defined clearly as they are the basis of any 'external' legal agreements.

7 Scope is formalized in the project specification.

The project specification may change during the course of the project for either internal (company) or external (customer) reasons. The company normally has to pay for changes made for internal reasons, the customer for those made due to external reasons.

8 Strategy defines how project management is going to meet its objectives.

Strategy defines how the organization is going to achieve the objectives of the project and reach the related measures of performance. It does this by:

• Defining the phases of the project - phases break the project down into time-based sections.

• Setting milestones - significant points when the project should be reviewed in terms of time, cost and quality.

How projects can be defined

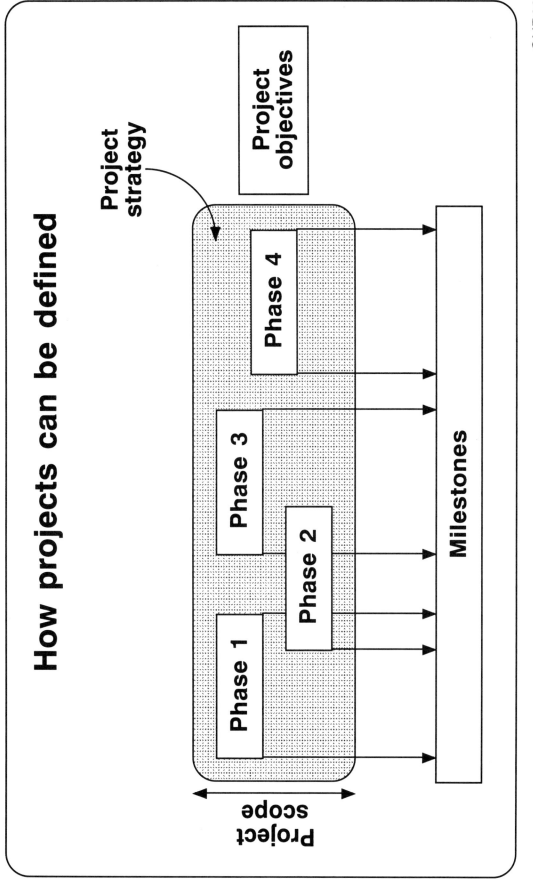

OHP89

How projects are planned

Points to make

1   There are four distinct reasons for planning projects.

  • to determine the cost and duration of the project;

  • to determine the level of resource that will be needed;

  • to allocate work and determine how the project will be monitored;

  • to assess the impact of any changes to the project.

2   There are several phases to the planning process.

3   Phase 1 - identify activities - the work breakdown structure.
Projects are often too complex to be controlled unless they are broken down into manageable portions. This is done by building a family tree which specifies the major tasks or sub-projects. Once this top-level family tree has been built, the major tasks or sub-projects are subdivided, until a manageable 'work package' is ultimately defined.

Once defined each work package is allocated its own objectives in terms of time, cost and quality.

4   Phase 2 - estimate times and resources.
Estimates of time and resource requirements are fundamental to project planning. They are rarely perfect, but can be made with an idea of how accurate they are likely to be - probabilistic estimates.

5   Phase 3 - identify relationships and dependencies.
Activities defined as part of a project will have some relationship with the other activities that are part of that same project. Sometimes one activity will have to be completed before another one can be begun. These are known as dependent activities.

The existence of dependent activities means that there will be a series of dependent activities which together determine the minimum possible time in which the project can be completed - the critical path.

6   Phase 4 - identify schedule constraints.
This involves comparing project requirements with available resources. If more resources are required than are available the project can either be declared:

  • Resource constrained - limited resources are available and hence the project will have to slip.

  • Time constrained - use up all the available resources before finding alternative 'threshold' resources.

7   Fix the schedule.

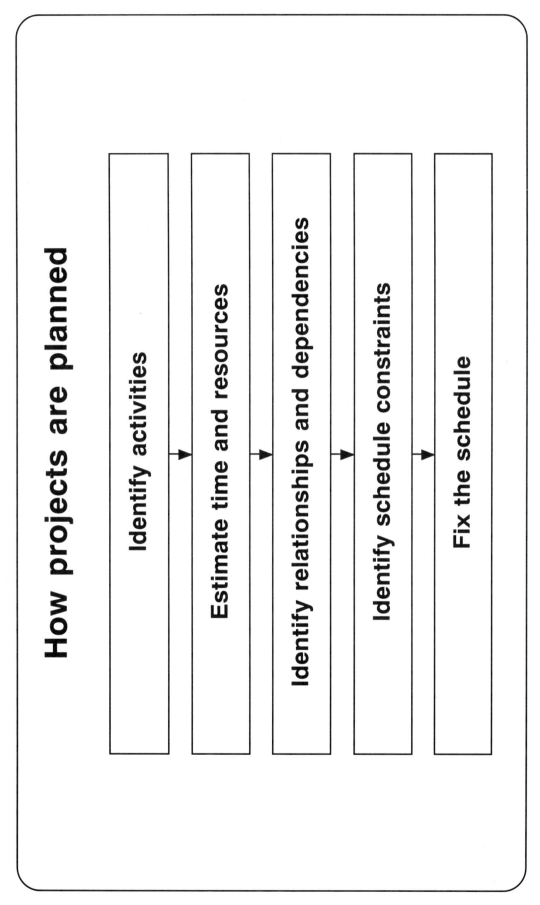

How projects are planned

Identify activities → Estimate time and resources → Identify relationships and dependencies → Identify schedule constraints → Fix the schedule

OHP90

How projects are controlled

Points to make

1   The process of project control involves three decisions.

2   How to monitor the project in order to check on its progress.
The main objectives of any project are usually defined in terms of cost, quality and time. Hence these are the things that need to be measured.

3   How to assess the performance of the project by comparing progress with the project plan.
Time can be monitored by comparing progress to plan. The planned times can be found on the project schedule.

Expected costs can also be estimated using the schedule. Normally few activities can be started immediately as most are dependent on other activities being completed. As the project progresses, more and more activities can be started. Then, towards the end of the project, fewer and fewer activities remain to be undertaken. Hence the cost profile of a project is normally an 'S' curve. Project costs can be compared against this curve.

4   Progress can be evaluated using earned value control.
Rather than measuring progress in terms of days of work completed, earned value control measures the value of work done. There are three important measures associated with earned value control:

- The budgeted cost of work scheduled (BCWS). This is the amount of work which should have been completed by a particular time.

- The budgeted cost of work performed (BCWP). This is the actual amount of work which has been completed by a particular time.

- The actual cost of work performed (ACWP). This is the actual expenditure which has been incurred as a result of the work completed by a particular time.

From these three measures, two variances which indicate deviation from plan can be calculated:

- Schedule variance (SV) = BCWP minus BCWS

- Cost variance (CV) = BCWP minus ACWP

5   How to intervene in the project in order to make the changes which will bring it back to plan.
When intervening in the project it is important to be aware of interactions, and/or the knock-on effects of any interactions.

How projects are controlled

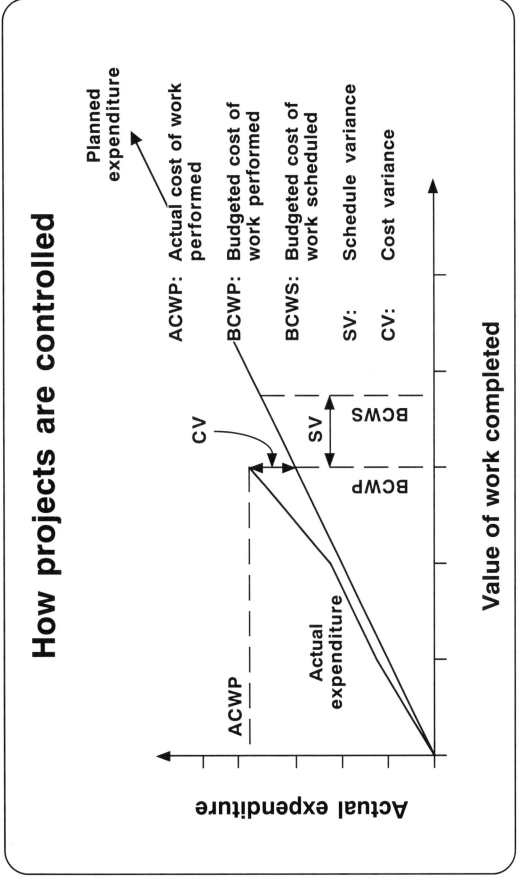

ACWP: Actual cost of work performed

BCWP: Budgeted cost of work performed

BCWS: Budgeted cost of work scheduled

SV: Schedule variance

CV: Cost variance

OHP91

Network analysis and how it can be used

Points to make

1 Project planning techniques are collectively known as 'network analysis'.

The simplest project planning and control technique is the Gantt chart. Other techniques include critical path analysis (CPA) and project evaluation and review technique (PERT).

2 Critical path analysis (CPA).

There are two ways in which CPA charts can be drawn - activities can be shown on the nodes (AoN) or on the arrows (AoA).

The advantages of the activity-on-node (AoN) method are:

* It is often easier to move from the basic logic of a project's relationships to a network diagram using the AoN method.

* AoN diagrams do not need dummy activities to maintain the logic of relationships.

* Most of the computer packages which are used in project planning and control use an AoN format.

3 The rules used for drawing CPA charts.

There are three basic rules that have to be followed when drawing CPA charts:

* Rule 1 - an event cannot be reached until all activities leading to it are complete.

* Rule 2 - no activity can start until its tail event is reached.

* Rule 3 - no two activities can have the same head and tail events.

4 CPA charts are designed to show diagrammatically the logical sequence in which activities have to take place.

The critical path is the one with the longest sequence of activities. It is called critical path because any delay in any of the activities on this path will delay the whole project.

By drawing the network diagram it is possible to: (a) identify the most important activities; (b) calculate the duration of the whole project; and (c) calculate slack or float - spare (excess) time on a given path. Doing this makes it possible to identify the earliest and latest start times for each activity.

5 Project Evaluation and Review Technique (PERT).

PERT was developed for the US Navy. It involves drawing a network diagram which specifies estimates for completing activities which are: (a) optimistic; (b) most likely; and (c) pessimistic.

6 Network analysis has to take account of resource constraints.

By doing so projects can be crashed. Crashing projects is the process of reducing the project timespan by: (a) overtime working; (b) additional resources; and (c) subcontracting.

The most cost-effective way of crashing networks is to crash the activity on the critical path with the lowest cost slope, where the cost slope is the cost per unit time of reducing each activity's duration.

Network analysis and how it can be used

Activity	Immediate predecessors	Duration (days)
Remove furniture (a)	None	1
Prepare bedroom (b)	a	2
Paint bedroom (c)	b	3
Prepare kitchen (d)	a	1
Paint kitchen (e)	d	2
Replace furniture (f)	c and e	1

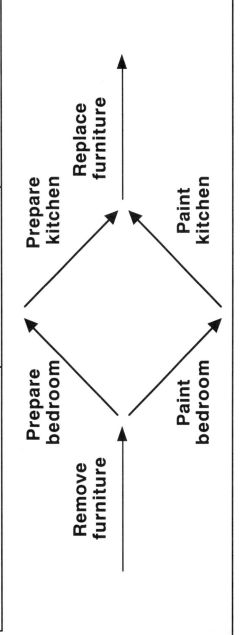

CHAPTER 17

QUALITY PLANNING AND CONTROL

Key question
• How can quality be defined?
• How can quality problems be diagnosed?
• What steps lead towards conformance to specification?
• How can statistical process control help quality planning and control?
• How can acceptance sampling help quality planning and control?

Topics covered
• The various definitions of quality.
• The perception-expectation gap theory of quality in operations.
• Quality characteristics of goods and services.
• 'Attributes' and 'variables' measures of quality, and quality standards.
• The use of statistical process control (SPC) in quality planning and control.
• The use of acceptance sampling plans (ASP) in quality planning and control.

Summary

How can quality be defined?
• In several ways. Among the approaches are the transcendent approach which views quality as meaning 'innate excellence', the manufacturing-based approach which views quality as being 'free of errors', the user-based approach which views quality as 'fit for purpose', the product-based approach which views quality as a 'measurable set of characteristics' and the value-based approach which views quality as a balance between 'cost and price'.
• The definition of quality used in this book combines all these approaches to define quality as 'consistent conformance to customers' expectations'.

How can quality problems be diagnosed?
• At a broad level quality is best modelled as the gap between customers' expectations concerning the product or service and their perceptions concerning the product or service.
• Modelling quality this way will allow the development of a diagnostic tool which is based around the perception-expectation gap. If such a gap exists it is likely to be caused by one or more of the gaps between factors which influence expectations and perceptions.
• There are four main gaps.
   The gap between the customer's specification and the operation's specification.
   The gap between the product or service concept and the way the organization has specified it.
   The gap between the way quality has been specified and the actual delivered quality.
   The gap between the actual delivered quality and the way the product or service has been described to the customer.
• It is the third gap (between the specification of quality and the actual quality delivered) which is of particular concern to operations managers.

What steps lead towards conformance to specification?
• Six steps, these are:
- define quality characteristics;
- decide how to measure each of the quality characteristics;
- set quality standards for each characteristic;
- control quality against these standards;
- find the correct cause of poor quality;
- continue to make improvements.
• Most quality planning and control involves sampling the operations performance in some way. Sampling can give rise to erroneous judgments. These can be classed as either Type I or Type II errors. Type I errors involve making corrections where none are needed. Type II errors involve not making corrections where they are in fact needed.

How can statistical process control help quality planning and control?
• Statistical process control (SPC) involves using control charts to track the performance of one or more quality characteristics in the operation. The power of control charting lies in its ability to set 'control limits' derived from the statistics of the natural variation of processes. These control limits are often set at ±3 standard deviations of the natural variation of the process samples.
• Control charts can be used either for attributes or variables. An attribute is a quality characteristic which has two states (for example, right or wrong). A variable is one which can be measured on a continuously variable scale.
• Process control charts allow operations managers to distinguish between the 'normal' variation inherent in any process and the variations which could be caused by the process going out of control.

How can acceptance sampling help quality planning and control?
• Acceptance sampling helps managers to understand the risks they are taking when they make decisions about a whole batch of products on the basis of a sample taken from that batch. The risks of any particular sampling plan are shown on its operating characteristic (OC) curve.
• Some of the assumptions within acceptance sampling (most notably that a certain level of defects are 'acceptable') are not looked on favourably by proponents of total quality management (see Chapter 20).

The various definitions of quality

Points to make

1   Quality is important for two reasons.

- It impacts all the other dimensions of performance.

- It contributes to increased profitability. Higher quality can lead to enhanced revenues and reduced costs.

2   There are five basic approaches to defining quality.

The transcendent approach views quality as synonymous with innate excellence. Quality is the absolute - the best possible in terms of the product or service's specification.

The manufacturing-based approach assumes quality is all about making or providing error-free products or services that conform exactly to their design specifications.

The user-based approach assumes quality is all about providing products or services that are fit for their purpose. The products or services should conform to the specification and do what the customer wants them to do.

The product-based approach views quality as a precise and measurable set of characteristics that are required to satisfy the customer.

The value-based approach takes the manufacturing definition one stage further and defines quality in terms of 'value'. The benefit the product or service provides versus price paid.

3   If quality is defined as 'consistent conformance to customers' expectations' these perspectives can be reconciled.

The use of the term 'conformance' emphasizes that a specification is needed (the manufacturing perspective).

The use of the term 'consistent' emphasizes that conformance is not ad hoc, but planned and controlled via a measurable set of product or service characteristics (the product-based perspective).

The use of the phrase 'customers' expectations' combines the user- and value-based perspectives.

4   Quality is deliberately defined in terms of expectations.

Defining quality in terms of wants would imply that everything the customer wants should be provided.

Defining quality in terms of needs would imply that only the customer's basic requirements should be satisfied.

Defining quality in terms of expectations implies that the customer should get what he or she believes is likely.

The various definitions of quality

- The transcendent approach views quality as synonymous with innate excellence.

- The manufacturing-based approach assumes quality is all about making or providing error-free products or services.

- The user-based approach assumes quality is all about providing products or services that are fit for their purpose.

- The product-based approach views quality as a precise and measurable set of characteristics.

- The value-based approach defines quality in terms of 'value'.

The perception-expectation gap theory of quality

Points to make

1 The problem with basing the definition of quality on customers' expectations is that customers' expectations vary.

Past experience, individual knowledge and history all serve to shape customers' expectations.

As a result each customer will have different expectations and so the perceived quality of a given product or service will vary from customer to customer.

This issue is further complicated by the fact that sometimes quality cannot be judged in a technical sense, so customers have to use proxy or surrogate measures.

2 The operation's and customer's views of quality have to be reconciled.

The greater the degree of fit between the customer's perception of how well the product has performed and his/her expectation of how well it should have performed, the better the perceived quality.

3 There are four basic reasons why there might be a mismatch between the customer's perceptions and expectations.

Gap 1 - The customer specification-operations specification gap:
- This is often due to a mismatch between the organization's own internal quality specification and the specification which is expected by the customer.

Gap 2 - The concept-specification gap:
- This is often due to a mismatch between the product or service concept and the way the organization has specified the quality of the product or service internally.

Gap 3 - The quality specification-actual quality gap:
- This is often due to a mismatch between the actual quality of the product or service provided by the operation and its internal quality specification.

Gap 4 - The actual quality-communicated image gap:
- This is often due to a mismatch between the organization's external communications or market image and the actual quality of the product of service delivered to the customer.

The perception-expectation gap

Gap	Action required to ensure high perceived quality	Main organizational responsibility
Gap 1	Ensure consistency between internal quality specification and the expectations of customers.	Marketing, operations, product/service development
Gap 2	Ensure internal specification meets its intended concept of design.	Marketing, operations, product/service development
Gap 3	Ensure actual product or service conforms to its internally specified quality level.	Operations
Gap 4	Ensure that promises made to customers concerning the product or service can really be delivered.	Marketing

Quality characteristics of goods and services

Points to make

1   The quality planning and control activity involves:

- Defining the quality characteristics of the product or service;

- Deciding how to measure each quality characteristic.

2   Defining the quality characteristics of the product or service.

What defines 'quality' for a given product or service will have been specified, at least implicitly, during the design of that product or service.

There are different categories of quality characteristic, including:

- Functionality - how well the product or service does the job for which it was intended.

- Appearance - aesthetic appeal, look, feel, sound and smell of the product or service.

- Reliability - consistency of product or service's performance over time.

- Durability - the total useful life of the product or service.

- Recovery - the ease with which problems with the product or service can be rectified or resolved.

- Contact - the nature of the person-to-person contacts that take place.

3   Deciding how to measure each quality characteristic.

If quality is to be controlled we need to be able to measure each quality characteristic. To do this we have to break down each general quality characteristic into its constituent elements.

This has to be done carefully because there is a danger that some of the meaning of the general quality characteristics will be lost during the process of disaggregation.

Quality characteristics of goods and services

- **Functionality** - how well the product or service does the job for which it was intended.

- **Appearance** - aesthetic appeal, look, feel, sound and smell of the product or service.

- **Reliability** - consistency of product or services performance over time.

- **Durability** - the total useful life of the product or service.

- **Recovery** - the ease with which problems with the product or service can be rectified or resolved.

- **Contact** - the nature of the person-to-person contacts that take place.

Attribute and variable measures and quality standards

Points to make

1 **Quality characteristics can be defined as attributes or variables.**
   Attributes are items that are assessed by judgment and are dichotomous (i.e. have two states).

   Variables are items that are measured on a continuous scale.

2 **In general, standards should be achievable, rather than absolute (perfection).**

3 **Once standards have been set, quality needs to be controlled against them.**
   To do this three decisions have to be taken:
   • Where in the operation should conformance be checked?

   • How often should conformance be checked?

   • How should conformance be checked?

4 **Where in the operation should conformance be checked?**
   There are three points at which conformance can be checked: (a) at the start of the process; (b) during the process; and (c) at the end of the process.

   There are also a number of times at which it is sensible to check conformance: (a) before a particularly costly part of the process; (b) before a series of processes during which checking might be difficult; (c) immediately after part of the process with a high defective rate or failure point; (d) before a part of the process that might conceal previous defects or problems; (e) before a 'point of no return', after which rectification and recovery might be impossible; (f) before potential damage or distress might be caused; and (g) before a change in functional responsibility.

5 **How often should conformance be checked?**
   Should every item be checked, or should a selection of items be checked (sampling)?

   In some cases it is not possible to check every item because doing so: (a) may be dangerous; (b) may destroy the product or service; and (c) will be very time consuming and therefore costly.

   Even if every item is checked, all the defects will not necessarily be found, because: (a) making the checks may be inherently difficult; (b) staff may become fatigued and therefore make mistakes; (c) quality measures may be unclear and the staff making the checks may not know precisely what to look for; and (d) the wrong information may be given.

   An alternative is sampling, but there are risks associated with it:
   • Type I errors - when a decision is made to do something and the situation does not warrant it.

   • Type II errors - when nothing is done, yet a decision to do something should be taken as the situation does warrant it.

6 **How should conformance be checked?**
   Most operations use statistical process control and/or acceptance sampling plans. Both of these approaches are based on sampling, rather than 100% inspection.

Attribute and variable measures of quality

Attributes	Variables
Defective or not defective?	Measured on a continuous scale.
Light bulb works or does not work.	Diameter of bulb.
Number of defects in a turbine blade.	Length of bar.

The use of statistical process control (SPC)

Points to make

1   **Statistical process control (SPC) is concerned with checking a product or service during its creation.**
    SPC can be used to identify if there is a problem during the 'creation process' so that the 'creation process' can be stopped and the problem rectified.

2   **A key tool in statistical process control (SPC) is the control chart.**
    The value of the control chart is that it allows quality to be monitored over a period of time in a predictive manner. Control charts help detect if a process is going out of control before it actually does so.

3   **Control charts are based on process variability.**
    There are two types of process variability:

    • Common cause variability - variability which can be reduced but never eliminated entirely.

    • Assignable variability - variability that can be eliminated because it can be assigned to particular, controllable, causes.

4   **Common cause variability is used to assess process capability.**
    Common cause variability can be used to establish whether the process under examination is capable of producing what it is being asked to produce.

5   **Control charts are designed to monitor whether assignable variability is increasing.**
    Control limits, which are loosely based on probability theory, are used to assess whether a given process should be stopped.

6   **Control charts can be drawn up for both attributes and variables.**

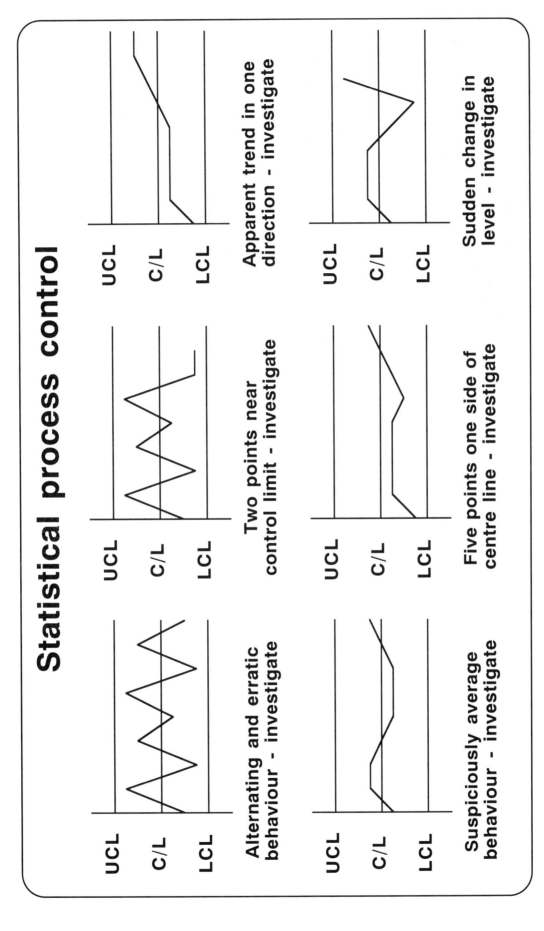

Statistical process control

OHP97

The use of acceptance sampling plans (ASP)

Points to make

1   Acceptance sampling is used to decide whether a given batch of work should be accepted or rejected.
Acceptance sampling is normally carried out using attributes rather than variables.

2   The acceptance sampling process involves:
• Taking 'n' items from a batch.

• Inspecting each item in the sample and recording how many are defective.

• Comparing the number of defective items with those allowed according to the sampling plan.

• Accepting or rejecting the batch depending on whether the number of defects found is greater or fewer than the number allowed under the plan.

3   As with all sampling schemes there are risks associated with acceptance sampling.
Type I errors are called the producer's risk. This is the risk of rejecting a batch which should actually be accepted.

Type II errors are called the consumer's risk. This is the risk of accepting a batch that should actually be rejected.

4   The consumer and producer risks for a given sampling plan are shown by that sampling plan's operating characteristic curve.

5   Sampling plans can be designed using tables.
The most common of these are BS6001 and Dodge Romig.

6   The major criticism of acceptance sampling is that it assumes that it is acceptable to produce a certain proportion of defective product.

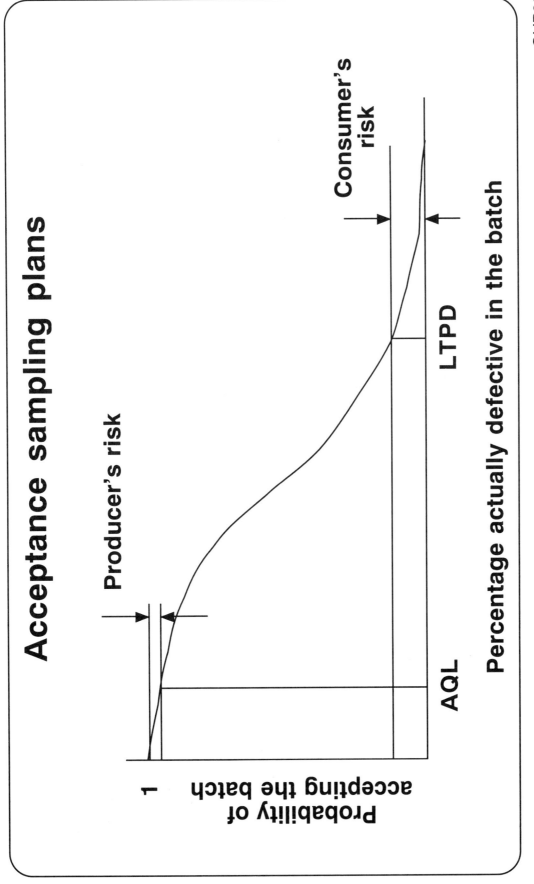

Acceptance sampling plans

OHP98

CHAPTER 18

OPERATIONS IMPROVEMENT

Key questions
- How can operations measure their performance in terms of the five performance objectives?
- How can operations managers prioritize improvement of performance objectives?
- What are the broad approaches to managing the rate of improvement?
- Where does business process re-engineering (BPR) fit into the improvement activity?
- What are the techniques of improvement?

Topics covered
- How operations can measure their performance in terms of the five performance objectives.
- The principles and stages of benchmarking.
- The way in which operations managers can quantify the importance of their significant competitive factors and their achieved performance using the importance-performance matrix.
- The two contrasting improvement strategies of continuous and breakthrough improvement.
- The business process re-engineering (BPR) approach to improvement.
- Some common techniques of operations improvement.

Summary

How can operations measure their performance in terms of the five performance objectives?
- It is unlikely that for any operation a single measure of performance will adequately reflect the whole of a performance objective. Usually operations have to collect a whole bundle of partial measures of performance.
- Each partial measure then has to be compared against some performance standard. There are four types of performance standard commonly used:
    - Historical standards which compare performance now against some time in the past.
    - Target performance standards which compare performance against some desired level of performance.
    - Competitive performance standards which compare performance against competitors' performance.
    - Absolute performance standards which compare performance against its theoretically perfect state.
- The process of benchmarking is often used as a means of obtaining competitor performance standards.

How can operations managers prioritize improvement of performance objectives?
- Improvement priorities can be determined by bringing together the relative importance of each performance objective or competitive factor as judged by customers, with the performance which the operation achieves as compared against competitors.
- The operation's judgment about both importance and performance can be consolidated on an 'importance-performance' matrix. Different areas on this matrix represent different relative degrees of importance.

What are the broad approaches to managing the rate of improvement?
- An organization's approach to improving its operation can be characterized as lying somewhere between the two extremes of 'pure' breakthrough improvement and 'pure' continuous improvement.

• Breakthrough improvement, which is sometimes called innovation-based improvement, sees the rate of improvement as occurring in a few infrequent but major and dramatic changes. Although such changes can be abrupt and volatile they often incorporate radical new concepts or technologies which can shift the performance of the operation significantly.

• Continuous improvement assumes a series of never-ending but smaller incremental improvement steps. This type of improvement is sometimes called *kaizen* improvement. Continuous improvement is gradual and constant and often utilizes collective group-based problem solving. It does not focus on radical changes but rather attempts to develop an ingrained momentum of improvement.

• It is claimed that compromises between these two types of improvement philosophy are possible. Organizations can improve by having occasional radical breakthroughs but utilizing a more incremental approach in between the major changes.

Where does business process re-engineering (BPR) fit into the improvement activity?

• BPR is a typical example of the radical approach to improvement. It attempts to redesign operations along customer-focused processes rather than on the traditional functional basis.

• BPR has been responsible for some radical improvement in operations performance but has also been criticized. The main criticisms are that it pays little attention to the rights of staff who are the victims of the 'down-sizing' which often accompanies BPR and that the radical nature of the change can strip out valuable experience from the operation.

What are the techniques of improvement?

• Many of the techniques described throughout this book could be considered improvement techniques, for example, statistical process control (SPC).

• Techniques often seen as 'improvement techniques' are,

   - input-output analysis which attempts to clarify the nature of transformation in processes.
   - flow charts which attempt to describe the nature of information flow and decision making within operations.
   - scatter diagrams which attempt to identify relationships and influences within the process.
   - cause-effect diagrams which structure the brainstorming which can help to reveal the root causes of problems.
   - Pareto diagrams which attempt to sort out the 'important few' causes from the 'trivial many' causes.

How operations can measure their performance

Points to make

1   **Before devising an improvement strategy managers need to know where they are.**
    Improvement priorities are determined partly by whether current performance is judged to be good, bad or indifferent. Performance measures are therefore a prerequisite to improvement.

2   **Performance measurement can be defined as the process of quantifying action.**
    Where measurement means the process of quantification and the performance of the operation is assumed to derive from actions taken by its members.

3   **The five basic performance measures for operations relate to the five performance objectives.**

4   **Market needs and expectations vary, as will the extent to which an operation meets these needs.**
    The market's requirements and the operation's performance also vary over time.

5   **Each performance objective can be broken down into sub-objectives.**
    This gives a hierarchy of performance measures.

6   **Managers need performance standards as well as performance measures.**
    There are various types of performance standard:

    • Historical standards which compare current and past performance. These show whether the organization is getting better or worse, but give no indication of whether performance should be regarded as satisfactory.

    • Target performance standards which are set arbitrarily to reflect some level of performance which is regarded as appropriate.

    • Competitor performance standards which compare the performance of the operation with that achieved by competitors. The advantage of competitor performance standards is that they relate performance directly to competitive ability.

    • Absolute performance standards which take performance to its theoretical limits. Although the target level may never be achieved it can provide motivation and direction.

How operations can measure their performance

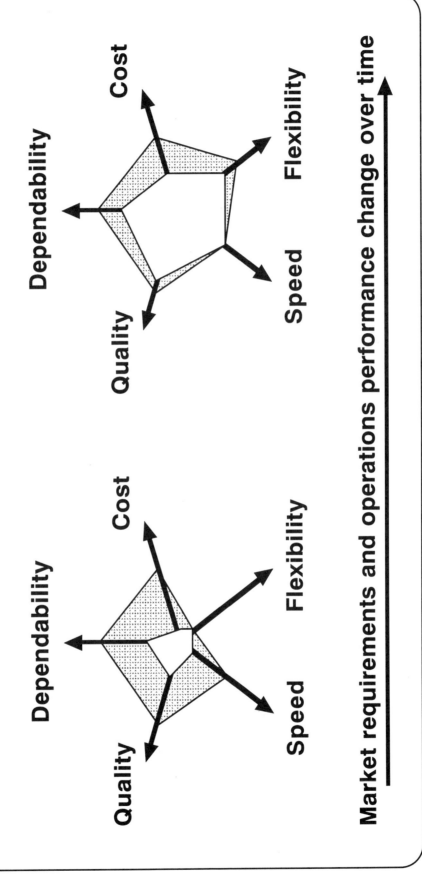

Market requirements and operations performance change over time

OHP99

The principles and stages of benchmarking

Points to make

1 Xerox used the term 'competitive benchmarking' to describe a process ...

Used by the manufacturing function to revitalize itself by comparing the features, assemblies and components of its products with those of its competitors.

2 Since Xerox first used the term it has broadened in meaning.

Benchmarking is no longer:

- restricted to the manufacturing function - its applicability to other functional areas is now recognized;

- confined only to manufacturing organizations - it has been used in services;

- practised only by experts and consultants - benchmarking exercises often involve a variety of staff.

3 The meaning of the term 'competitive' has also widened.

It is now taken to mean benchmarking to gain competitive advantage, rather than benchmarking in the sense of direct comparison with competitors.

4 There are various types of benchmarking.

Internal benchmarking - comparison between operations or parts of operations which are within the same total organization.

External benchmarking - comparison between operations which are parts of different organizations.

Non-competitive benchmarking - benchmarking against operations which are not direct competitors.

Competitive benchmarking - benchmarking against operations which are direct competitors.

Performance benchmarking - comparing levels of achieved performance.

Practice benchmarking - comparing how performance is actually achieved (the way things are done).

5 There are three basic reasons why companies benchmark.

Benchmarking is carried out:

- partly to determine how well an organization is performing;

- partly to help set performance standards;

- partly to help identify new ways of doing things.

The principles and stages of benchmarking

- Benchmarking is carried out:

  - partly to determine how well an organization is performing.

  - partly to help set performance standards.

  - partly to help identify new ways of doing things.

The importance-performance matrix

Points to make

1 Two factors influence which performance objectives should be focused on.

- The needs and preferences of customers.

- The performance and activities of competitors.

2 The needs and preferences of customers.

What customers think is important should also be what the operation thinks is important.

It is often useful to categorize performance objectives according to whether they are:

- Order-winning criteria - those factors which directly win business for the operation.

- Order-qualifying criteria - those factors which may not win extra business for the operation, but can cause the operation to lose business if performance falls below a certain level.

- Less-important factors - those factors which are relatively unimportant to the business.

Extra discrimination can be achieved by breaking these down into three, three-point scales, representing strong, medium and weak positions.

3 The performance and activities of competitors.

If the operation is not as good as, or better than its competitors, it will not win business. Hence achieved performance can be assessed using a three-point scale - better than, the same as or worse than.

Again more discrimination can be introduced by breaking each of these three categories down into three sub-categories.

4 The importance-performance matrix is based on these two nine-point scales.

The importance-performance matrix helps identify:

- whether performance is satisfactory (the appropriate zone);

- whether performance needs improving (the improve zone);

- whether performance needs improving quickly (the urgent action zone);

- whether performance is better than necessary (the excess zone).

5 The importance-performance matrix is valuable for two reasons.

- It helps to discriminate between many factors which may be in need of improvement.

- The exercise gives purpose and structure to the debate on improvement priorities.

The importance-performance matrix

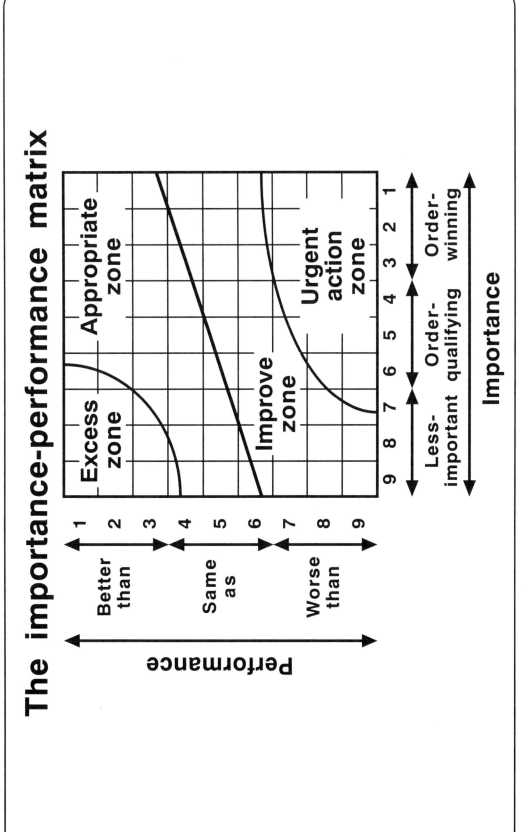

OHP101

Continuous and breakthrough improvement strategies

Points to make

1 There are two basic improvement strategies - continuous and breakthrough.

2 Continuous improvement (kaizen) strategies are based on small, frequent, incremental steps.

The major advantage of this strategy is that small step can follow small step after small step.

The size of the step is not important. What matters is that kaizen is an ongoing process. Hence maintaining momentum is the key.

3 The Deming cycle is a key concept in the kaizen process.

The Deming cycle consists of four cyclical steps:

- Plan - decide how performance could be improved.

- Do - implement the plan.

- Check - evaluate the improvements to see whether they have worked.

- Act - consolidate the improvements.

4 Breakthrough (innovation-based) improvement involves major changes in the way the operation works.

These changes can have a major impact on performance if implemented successfully, but:

- are often expensive;

- usually require major investment;

- often disrupt the operation;

- can be difficult to realize quickly.

5 The difference between breakthrough improvement and continuous improvement.

Breakthrough improvement places high value on creative solutions. It encourages free thinking and individualism. It fosters an approach which does not accept constraints on what is possible.

Continuous improvement is less ambitious, at least in the short term. It stresses adaptability, teamwork and attention to detail. It is not radical, rather it builds upon the wealth of accumulated experience within the operation itself, often relying on the people in the operation to improve it.

6 Breakthrough improvement and continuous improvement strategies are not mutually exclusive.

It is possible to combine the two approaches within a single operation.

Continuous and breakthrough improvement

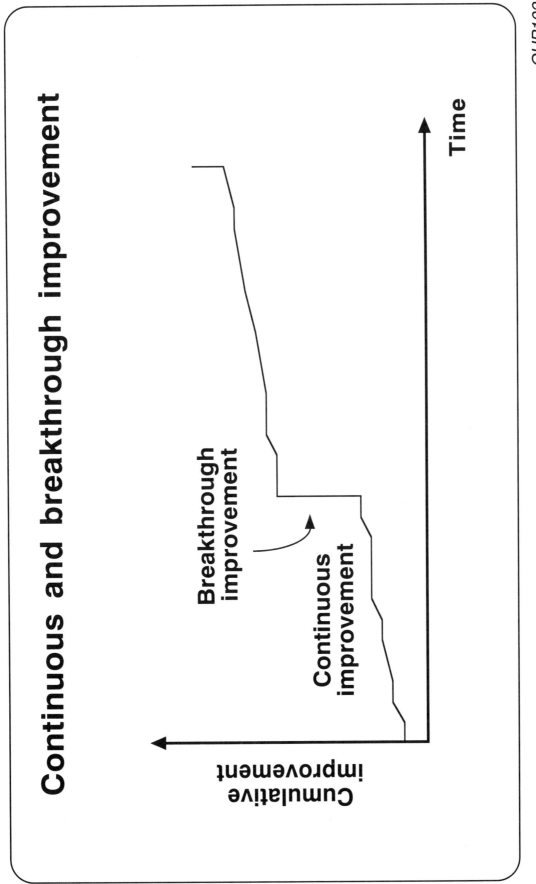

OHP102

The business process re-engineering approach

Points to make

1 Business process re-engineering (BPR) is a popular breakthrough improvement strategy.

2 BPR blends a number of operations management ideas.
It is often the potential of information technology that makes radical improvement possible, however.

3 BPR involves thinking about the natural flows of information in organizations.
Rather than how best to structure the functions.

4 The basic principles of BPR:
- Rethink business processes in a cross-functional manner which organizes work around the natural flow of information (or materials or customers). This means organizing around outcomes of a process rather than the tasks which go into it.

- Strive for dynamic improvements in the performance by radically rethinking and redesigning the process.

- Have those who use the output from a process perform the process. Check to see if all internal customers can be their own supplier rather than depending on another function in the business to supply them.

- Put decision points where the work is performed. Do not separate those who do the work from those who control and manage the work.

5 BPR is not without its critics.
Three criticisms in particular appear to have some validity
- BPR is often treated as the latest management fad by some managers and as a cure-all for every problem. It is like, say the critics, attempting major surgery on every ailment even those which would cure themselves naturally with some simple physiotherapy.
- BPR is merely an excuse for getting rid of staff. Companies wishing to 'down-size' (that is, reduce numbers of staff within an operation) are using BPR as an excuse. This puts the short-term interests of the shareholders of the company above either their longer-term interests or the interests of the company's employees.
- A combination of radical redesign together with downsizing can mean that the essential core of experience is lost from the operation. This leaves it vulnerable to any environmental changes since it no longer has the knowledge and experience of how to cope with unexpected changes.

Business process re-engineering

Functional structure

Customers

↑ ↑ ↑

Function 1	Function 2	Function 3

↓ ↓ ↓

Suppliers

Process structure

Customers

↑ ↑ ↑

Process 1	←
Process 2	
Process 3	→

↑ ↑ ↑

Suppliers

Common techniques for process improvement

Points to make

1 There are various tools and techniques that can be used during the improvement process.

2 **Input/output analysis.**
Three tasks have to be completed to build an input/output model:

- The inputs to and outputs from the process have to be identified.

- The source of the inputs and the destination of the outputs have to be identified.

- The requirements of the internal customers who are served by the outputs of the process have to be clarified.

3 **Flow charts.**
Flow charts provide a detailed understanding of those parts of the process where a flow occurs.

They use two symbols to record the information in a logical format:

- A rectangular box is used to denote an action.

- A diamond-shaped box is used to highlight where in the process questions have to be answered or decisions made.

4 **Scatter diagrams.**
Scatter diagrams are a quick and simple method of identifying whether there appears to be a connection between two sets of data.

It is important to note that scatter diagrams only indicate that there may be some connection They do not demonstrate cause and effect.

5 **Cause-effect diagrams.**
Cause-effect diagrams help identify the root cause of a problem, by asking what, when, where, how and why type questions.

Cause-effect diagrams are also known as Ishikawa, or fish bone diagrams, because they were 'invented' by Ishikawa and end up looking like fish bones.

6 **Pareto diagrams.**
Pareto diagrams are a useful way of distinguishing between what is important and what is less important. They focus on identifying which problems occur frequently.

7 **Why-why analysis.**
Why-why analysis is a simple questioning technique designed to help identify what is at the root of an issue. Basically the process involves asking why, until no more "whys" can be asked.

Common techniques for process improvement

Input/output analysis	**Flow charts**	**Scatter diagrams**
Cause-effect diagrams	**Pareto diagrams**	**Why-why analysis**

CHAPTER 19

FAILURE PREVENTION AND CONTROL

Key questions
• Why do operations fail?
• How is failure measured?
• How can failure and potential failure be detected and analysed?
• How can operations improve their reliability?
• How should operations recover when failure does occur?

Topics covered
• Why systems fail.
• The various ways in which failure is measured.
• How failure and potential failure is detected and analysed to find its root cause.
• How operations improve their reliability to try to prevent failure - trying to engineer-out failure and the maintenance of facilities.
• Recovery strategies for dealing with failure - getting it very right the second time.

Summary
Why do operations fail?
• There are three major reasons why operations fail. The first is that the goods or services which are supplied to the operation themselves are faulty. The second reason is that something is happening within the operation, either because there is an overall failure in its design, because one or more of the physical facilities break down, or because there is human error. The third reason is that the customers themselves may cause failure through their incompetent handling of goods or services. Even so this is the responsibility of the management of the operation.
• Remember though, that not all failures are equally serious and attention is usually directed at those which have the most impact on the operation or its customers.

How is failure measured?
• There are three ways of measuring failure. 'Failure rates' indicate how often a failure is likely to occur. 'Reliability' measures the chances of a failure occurring. 'Availability' is the amount of available and useful operating time after taking account of failures.
• Failure over time is often represented as a failure curve. The most common form of this is the so called 'bath tub curve' which shows the chance of failure being greater at the beginning and end of life of a system or part of a system.

How can failure and potential failure be detected and analysed?
• Failure detection and analysis involves putting mechanisms into place which sense some kind of failure has occurred and then analyses the failure to try and understand its root causes.
• Failure detection mechanisms include in-process checks, machine diagnostic checks, point-of-departure interviews, phone surveys, focus groups, complaint cards or feedback sheets, and questionnaires.
• Failure analysis mechanisms include accident investigation, product liability, complaint analysis, critical incident analysis, and failure mode and effect analysis (FMEA).

How can operations improve their reliability?

• There are four major methods of improving reliability.

  Designing out the fail points in the operation.

  Building redundancy into the operation.

  'Fail-safeing' some of the activities of the operation.

  Maintenance of the physical facilities in the operation.

• Maintenance is the most common way operations attempt to improve their reliability.

• There are three broad approaches to maintenance. The first is running all facilities until they breakdown and then repairing them, the second is regularly maintaining the facilities even if they have not broken down, the third is to monitor facilities closely to try and predict when breakdowns might occur.

• Two specific approaches to maintenance have been particularly influential. These are total productive maintenance (TPM) and reliability centred maintenance. (RCM).

How should operations recover when a failure does occur?

• Recovery can be enhanced by a systematic approach to discovering what has happened to cause failure, acting to inform, contain, and follow-up the consequences of failure, learning to find the root cause of failure and preventing it taking place again, and planning to avoid the failure occurring in the future.

• The idea of 'business continuity' planning is probably the most common form of recovery planning.

Why systems fail

Points to make

1 Mistakes are inevitable so there is always a chance that systems will fail.
Accepting that failure will occur is not the same as ignoring it.

2 Not all failures are equally serious.
Some types and/or levels of failure can be tolerated. Organizations therefore need to discriminate between failures.

3 Systems fail for many different reasons.
These reasons can be classified according to the source of the failure.

4 Failures which are caused by the organization.
Such failures might be due to:

- Faults in the overall design of the operation. Perhaps demand was not accurately predicted, or maybe customer requirements were not translated into adequate designs.

- Problems with facilities, including machines, equipment and buildings.

- Problems with staff. Failures due to staff can be split into two categories: (a) errors in judgment; and (b) violations - failure to obey the rules.

5 Failures which are caused by the materials or information which are the inputs to the organization.
Such failures might be caused by the organization's suppliers, who may fail to supply the right goods or services at the right time, or in the right quantity, or at the right quality.

The more an operation relies on suppliers of materials or services, the more it is liable to failure which is caused by missing or substandard inputs.

6 Failures which are caused by the actions of customers.
Failures can occur if customers misuse the product or service. As a result most operations have to educate their customers.

7 Failures are not all bad.
Failures provide an opportunity to learn and to improve the product or service.

Why systems fail

Supply failures

Failures inside the operation

- Design failures
- Facilities failures
- Staff failures

Customer failures

OHP105

The various ways in which failure is measured

Points to make

1   Failure can be measured in three ways:

- Failure rates.

- Reliability.

- Availability.

2   Failure rates measure how often a failure occurs.

Failure rates are usually calculated as the number of failures over a period of time. They are sometimes expressed as a percentage.

Failure rates can be calculated using actual operating or test data.

3   The likelihood of failure changes over time.

The likelihood of a failure occurring at a particular point in time can be represented as a probability distribution. The most common representation is the 'bath tub' curve which has three stages:

- The infant-mortality or 'early-life' stage where failure occurs mainly because of defective parts or improper use.

- The 'normal-life' stage when the failure rate is usually low and reasonably constant. Failures in the 'normal-life' stage are usually due to normal random failure.

- The 'wear-out' stage when the failure rate increases as the part approaches the end of its working life. Failures in the 'wear-out' stage are usually due to the ageing and deterioration of parts.

4   Reliability measures the chances of a failure occurring.

Reliability measures the ability of a system, product or service to perform as expected over time.

Reliability decreases rapidly:

- the more components the product or service has;

- the greater the interdependence of the components.

A useful measure of reliability is mean time between failures.

5   Availability measures the amount of useful operating time that is available.

An operation is not available if it has either failed or is being repaired following failure.

How failure is measured

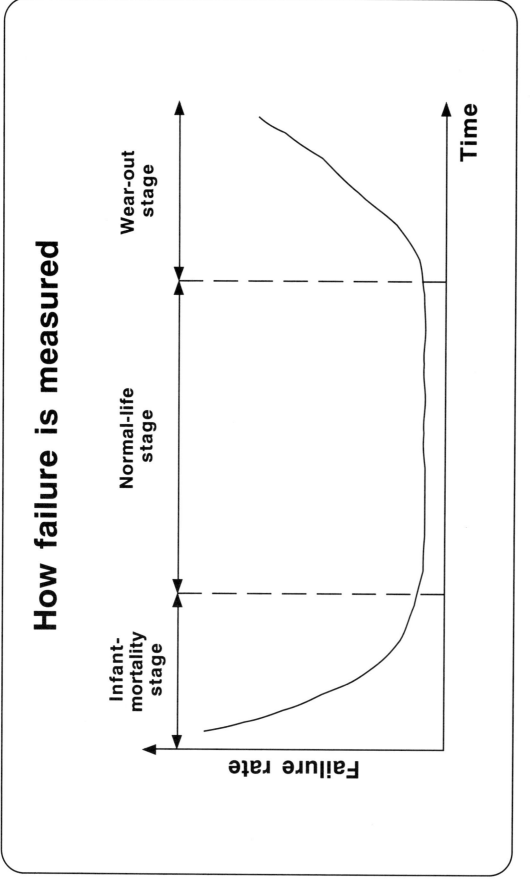

How failure is detected and analysed to find its root cause

Points to make

1 **Given that failures will occur operations need to put two things in place:**
   • mechanisms to ensure that a failure is recognized when it has occurred;

   • procedures which ensure that the root cause of the failure is identified and eliminated.

2 **Mechanisms to ensure that a failure is recognized when it has occurred.**
   Many mechanisms to ensure that failures are recognized are available. Some of the more common are:
   • In-process checks - devices used to monitor the machine or system as the product or service is being produced or delivered.

   • Machine-diagnostic checks - running machines through predetermined sequences of activities to check whether failure occurs.

   • Point-of-departure interviews - interviews used to check whether the product or service is acceptable once it has been delivered.

   • Phone surveys.

   • Focus groups - small groups of customers who are asked to comment on some aspect of a product or service.

   • Complaint cards or feedback sheets.

   • Questionnaires.

3 **Procedures which ensure that the root cause of the failure is identified and eliminated.**
   Collectively such procedures are called failure analysis. Some of the more common methods include:
   • Accident investigation - used mainly to investigate major national disasters.

   • Product liability - ensures product traceability so that the root cause of any failure can be corrected in all products.

   • Complaint analysis - a cheap and easily available source of information. Complaints are often only the 'tip of the iceberg', but they are valuable because they are unsolicited.

   • Critical incident analysis - ask customers to identify what they found particularly satisfying or particularly dissatisfying about a given product or service.

   • Failure mode-and-effect analysis - a systematic procedure built around the following three questions: (a) what is the likelihood that failure will occur; (b) what would the consequences of the failure be; and (c) how likely is it that such a failure would be detected before it affects the customer? Based on the answer to these three questions a 'risk priority number' (RPN) is assigned to each type of failure. Hence priorities can be established.

   • Fault-tree analysis - a logical procedure which starts with a failure and works backwards.

How failure is detected and analysed

- Failure detection mechanisms include:

  - in-process checks;

  - machine-diagnostic checks;

  - point-of-departure interviews.

- Failure analysis procedures include:

  - accident investigation;

  - failure mode-and-effect analysis;

  - fault-tree analysis.

How operations improve their reliability to prevent failure

Points to make

1   Operations can improve their reliability in a number of ways thereby preventing failure.

- By designing out the fail points in the operation - using 'process flow design' methods to redesign the operation.
- Building redundancy into the operation - introducing a back-up in case of failure. This is usually an expensive solution and hence only adopted when failure is critical.
- 'Fail-safeing' some of the activities in the operation. Mistakes are inevitable. *Poka-yokes* or fail-safeing devices seek to prevent them from happening. They are usually simple and cheap.
- Maintenance of the physical facilities in the operation. Benefits include: (a) enhanced safety; (b) increased reliability; (c) higher quality; (d) lower operating costs; and (e) longer lifespan; and (f) higher end value.

2   There are three basic approaches to the maintenance of facilities.

- Run to breakdown (RTB) - involves running a machine until breakdown and then repairing it.
- Preventative maintenance (PM) - attempts to eliminate or reduce the chances of failure by servicing the facilities at preplanned intervals.
- Condition-based maintenance (CBM) - attempts to perform maintenance when the facilities require it.

3   Most operations use mixed maintenance strategies.

Mixed maintenance strategies involve using different strategies in different circumstances. Run to breakdown is cheap and appropriate if the repair is relatively straightforward (and failure is not serious). Preventative maintenance should be used when the cost of unplanned failure is high. Condition-based maintenance should be used when maintenance is expensive.

4   There is a trade-off between breakdown and preventative maintenance.

The more frequently preventative maintenance is carried out the smaller the chance of breakdown. Therefore we want to set the balance between breakdown and preventative maintenance so that the total cost of maintenance is minimized.

5   The relationship between amount of maintenance and cost is not a straightforward one.

Often it is assumed that maintenance has to be carried out by skilled personnel. This is not always the case. Maintenance could be carried out by process owners, assuming this will not have a negative impact on productivity. Hence preventative maintenance can be cheaper than it first appears. Especially if it is carried out just before a breakdown is likely to occur - as predicted by a failure distribution.

6   Total productive maintenance is a relatively recent development.

Total productive maintenance (TPM) has five goals: (a) to improve equipment effectiveness; (b) to achieve autonomous maintenance; (c) to plan maintenance; (d) to train all staff in relevant maintenance skills; and (e) to try to eliminate the need for any maintenance by identifying root causes to all problems.

7   Reliability centred maintenance aims to reduce the impact of failure.

How operations improve their reliability

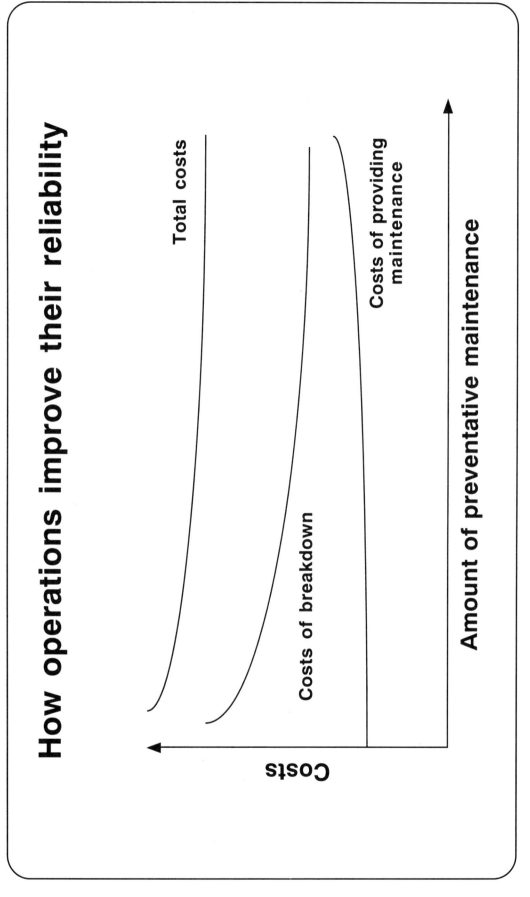

Total costs

Costs of breakdown

Costs of providing maintenance

Costs

Amount of preventative maintenance

OHP108

Recovery strategies for dealing with failure

Points to make

1 **All types of operation can benefit from well planned recovery.**
In fact well-planned recovery can enhance customer satisfaction. Customers accept that things sometimes go wrong. Once they have, the issue for the customer is - how well did the operation put them right?

2 **There are four stages to failure planning.**
Discover:
- What exactly has happened?

- Who will it affect?

- Why has it happened?

Act:
- Tell significant people what you propose to do.

- Contain the effects of the failure.

- Follow-up and check that the failure really has been contained.

Learn - identify the root cause of the failure and, if possible, engineer out the problem.

Plan - formally incorporate lessons from previous failures.

3 **The growing field of business continuity.**
Many of the ideas behind failure, failure prevention and recovery are incorporated into the growing field of business continuity. Business continuity aims to help operations avoid and recover from disasters while keeping the business growing.

Recovery strategies for dealing with failure

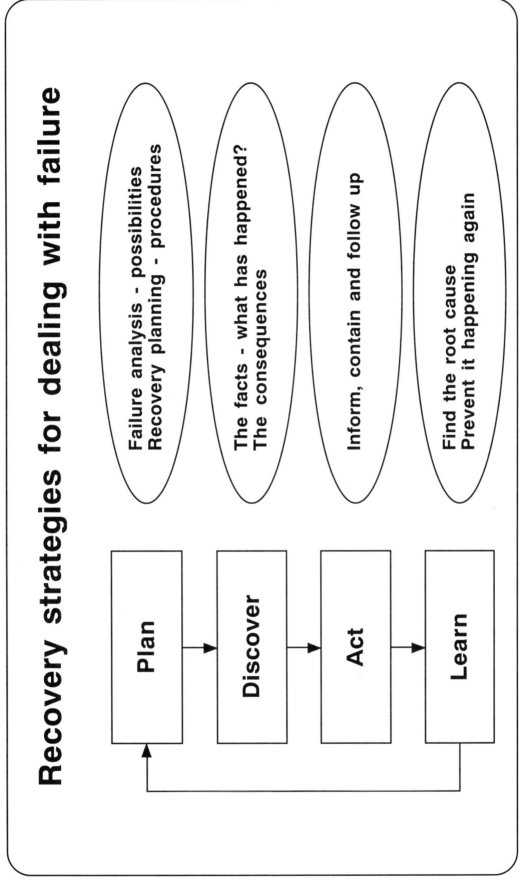

Plan	Failure analysis - possibilities Recovery planning - procedures
Discover	The facts - what has happened? The consequences
Act	Inform, contain and follow up
Learn	Find the root cause Prevent it happening again

CHAPTER 20

TOTAL QUALITY MANAGEMENT

Key questions
• Where did the idea of total quality management (TQM) come from?
• What are the main differences between traditional quality management and TQM?
• What is the role of ISO 9000 in TQM?
• What are the main implementation issues in TQM initiatives?
• How do quality awards and models contribute towards TQM?

Topics covered
• The origins of TQM and the significant 'gurus' who contributed to it.
• The differences between traditional approaches to quality and TQM.
• The ISO 9000 approach to quality management.
• How quality awards seek to promote TQM.

Summary
Where did the idea of total quality management (TQM) come from?
• Although the origins of total quality management go back to the 1940s and 1950s the term was first used formally in 1957 by Feigenbaum. Many authorities have contributed to the development of the idea. These authorities include Feigenbaum, Deming, Juran, Ishikawa, Taguchi and Crosby.
• The emphasis placed on various aspects of total quality management varies between the authorities, but the general thrust of their arguments is similar.
• Total quality management can be seen as being an extension of the traditional approach to quality. Inspection based quality control was replaced by the concept of quality assurance which in turn has been superseded by TQM.

What are the main differences between traditional quality management and TQM?
• TQM puts customers at the forefront of quality decision making. Customers' needs and expectations are always considered first in measuring achieved quality.
• TQM takes an organization-wide perspective. It holds that all parts of the organization have the potential to make a positive contribution to quality.   Central to this idea is the concept of the internal customer-supplier chain.
• TQM places considerable emphasis on the role and responsibilities of every member of staff within an organization to influence quality. It often encourages the idea of empowering individuals to improve their own part of the operation.
• The implied cost models of TQM are very different from those used in traditional approaches to quality. Traditionally the emphasis was usually placed on finding an 'optimum' amount of quality effort which minimized the costs associated with quality. By contrast, TQM emphasizes the balance between different types of quality costs. It argues that by increasing the amount of cost and effort placed on prevention there will be a more than equivalent reduction in other costs. This idea is often summarized on the phrase 'right first time'.
• TQM also places a heavy emphasis on the ideas of problem solving and continuous improvement dealt with in Chapter 18.

What is the role of ISO 9000 in TQM?
• ISO 9000 and associated standards are concerned with the systems and procedures which support quality. These are intended to assure purchasers of products and services that they have been produced in a way which meets customer requirements.

• ISO 9000 has received some criticism as being over bureaucratic and inflexible.

What are the main implementation issues in TQM initiatives?
• A number of factors appear to be influential in ensuring the success of TQM initiatives. These are as follows:
- the existence of a fully worked out quality strategy;
- top management support;
- a steering group to guide the initiative;
- group-based improvement;
- an adequate recognition and rewards scheme ;
- an emphasis on appropriate training.

How do quality awards and models contribute towards TQM?
• By providing a focused structure for organizations to assess their own quality management and improvement efforts.
• A number of organizations have attempted to encourage TQM by the award of prizes and certificates. The best known of these are the Deming Prize, the Malcolm Baldrige National Quality Award, and, in Europe, the European Quality Award (EQA).
• The EQA is based on a nine-point model which distinguishes between the 'enablers' of quality and the 'results' of quality. This is often now used as a self-certification model

The origins of TQM and the gurus who contributed to it

Points to make

1   The notion of TQM was introduced by Feigenbaum in 1957.
The concepts build on the work of several other quality gurus, however.

2   W. Edwards Deming.
Deming's basic thesis is that quality and productivity increase as process variability (the unpredictability of the process) decreases.

His philosophy is summarized in 14 points: (a) create consistency of purpose; (b) adopt the new philosophy; (c) cease dependence on inspection; (d) end awarding of business based on price; (e) improve constantly the system of production and service; (f) institute training on the job; (g) institute leadership; (h) drive out fear; (i) break down barriers between departments; (j) eliminate slogans and exhortations; (k) eliminate quotas or work standards; (l) give people pride in their job; (m) institute education and a self-improvement programme; and (n) put everyone to work to accomplish it.

3   Joseph Juran.
Juran tried to get organizations to move away from the traditional manufacturing-based view of quality as 'conformance to specification' to a more user-based approach 'fitness for use'.

He was concerned about impact of individual workers, as well as management.

4   Kaoru Ishikawa.
Ishikawa is credited with originating the concepts of quality circles and cause-and-effect diagrams.

He saw worker participation as key to the successful implementation of TQM.

5   Genichi Taguchi.
Taguchi was concerned with engineering-in quality through the optimization of product design.

He developed the 'quality loss function' which seeks to describe the loss to society a product or service can cause through warranty costs, customer complaints, and loss of customer goodwill.

6   Phillip Crosby.
Crosby is best known for his work on the cost of quality. He argues that many firms do not know how much they spend on quality - either putting it right or getting it wrong.

Crosby summarized his philosophy in the five absolutes of quality management: (a) quality is conformance to requirements; (b) prevention not appraisal; (c) the performance standard must be 'zero defects'; (d) measure the 'price of non-conformance' (PONC); and (e) there is no such thing as a quality problem.

Crosby's implementation plan for a quality improvement programme consists of 14 steps: (a) establish management commitment; (b) form interdepartmental quality teams; (c) establish quality measurement; (d) evaluate the cost of quality; (e) establish quality awareness; (f) instigate corrective action; (g) ad hoc committee for the zero defects programme; (h) supervisor employee training; (i) hold a zero defects day; (j) employee goal setting; (k) error cause removal; (l) recognition for meeting or exceeding goals; (m) establish quality councils; and (n) do it again.

The quality gurus

Philip Crosby	**Quality is free - the optimum is zero defects.**
W. Edwards Deming	**Deming's 14 points.** **How to use statistics.**
Armand Feigenbaum	**Total quality control.**
Kaoru Ishikawa	**Quality circles and cause and effect diagrams.**
Joseph Juran	**Quality as fitness for use, rather than conformance to specification.**
Genichi Taguchi	**Loss function.** **Minimize variation.**

Traditional approaches to quality and TQM

Points to make

1   TQM is a philosophy, a way of thinking and working, that is concerned with meeting the needs and expectations of customers.
It attempts to move the focus of quality away from being a purely operations activity into a major concern for the whole organiation. Through TQM, quality becomes the responsibility of all departments, sections and people in the organization.

2   TQM espouses the process of continuous improvement.

3   TQM is an extension of quality control.
Originally quality was achieved by inspection - screening out defects before they were noticed by customers. Quality control developed a more systematic way of doing this. Quality assurance widened the responsibility for quality to include functions other than direct operations and made more use of sophisticated statistical techniques. TQM includes all of the above, but is a more comprehensive approach for a variety of reasons.

4   TQM covers all parts of the organization.
A powerful TQM concept is that of internal customers and suppliers, which recognizes that everyone is both a customer and a supplier of someone else. This notion is captured in the idea of a service-level agreement which specifies what each customer wants (needs) from his supplier. Service-level agreements make explicit the fact that, if the external customer is to be satisfied, all internal customers have to be satisfied. They also make explicit the fact that everyone can contribute to quality and that a failure in any one part of the chain will ultimately be passed on to the final customer.

5   TQM involves more than simply avoiding failures.
TQM encourages people to identify how they can enhance the service they provide. This has implications for management style. TQM will not work in organizations where people are blamed for the mistakes they make.

6   TQM involves seeing things from the customer's point of view.
For TQM to work everyone has to understand the needs of their customers and put these needs at the forefront of decision making.

7   TQM considers all costs of quality.
There are four costs of quality: (a) prevention costs - the costs incurred in trying to prevent problems, failures and errors occurring in the first place; (b) appraisal costs - the costs associated with controlling quality to check to see if problems or errors have occurred during and after the creation of the product or service; (c) internal failure costs - the costs associated with errors which are dealt with inside the operation; and (d) external failure costs - the costs associated with an error going out of the operation to a customer.

Traditionally it was assumed that an 'optimum' level of spend can be identified because failure costs decrease as the money spent on appraisal and prevention increases. This model was been criticized because: (a) it assumes that failure (poor quality) is acceptable; (b) it assumes that costs are known and measurable; and (c) it implies that prevention is inevitably costly. In reality what seems to happen as TQM is implemented is that internal, then external, failure costs fall. As a result confidence grows and appraisal costs reduce. Finally, as the operation fully takes on the new way of working, prevention costs also fall.

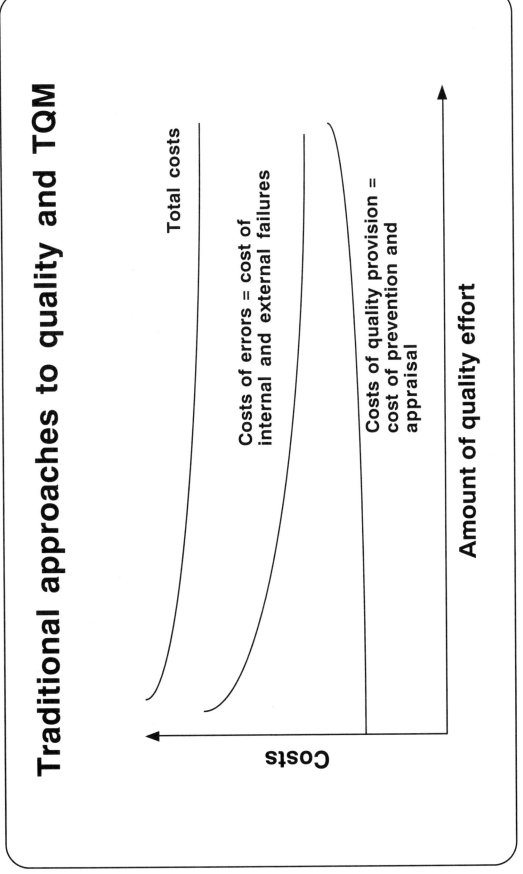

Traditional approaches to quality and TQM

Total costs

Costs of errors = cost of internal and external failures

Costs of quality provision = cost of prevention and appraisal

Costs

Amount of quality effort

OHP111

The ISO 9000/BS5750 approach to quality management

Points to make

1 Quality systems consist of three levels.

Level 1 - company quality manual. A concise summary of the company's quality management policy, quality system, objectives and organization.

Level 2 - procedures manual. A description of the systems, functions, structures and responsibilities of each department.

Level 3 - work instructions. A summary of the specifications and detailed methods for performing work activities.

Sometimes there can be a fourth level - a database containing all other reference documents.

2 The internationally recognized quality system is ISO 9000.

ISO 9000 registration requires third-party assessment of a company's quality standards and procedures. Regular audits are also conducted to ensure that the systems do not decay.

The purpose of ISO 9000 is to provide assurance to purchasers of products and services that the products or services have been produced in a way that meets their requirements.

The UK equivalent of ISO 9000 is BS5750.

3 The advantages of ISO 9000:

- It provides a useful discipline for the operation.

- It has benefits in terms of reduced numbers of errors, reduced customer complaints and reduced costs of quality.

- The ISO 9000 audit is a generally accepted standard. Companies that are ISO 9000 accredited are rarely subject to 'extra' customer audits.

- Adopting ISO 9000 procedures can lead to the identification of existing procedures which are unnecessary and can therefore be eliminated.

- Gaining ISO 9000 status shows the company is serious about quality. This has marketing benefits.

4 The disadvantages of ISO 9000:

- The emphasis on standards encourages management by the manual.

- Choosing which of the various standards to apply for is not easy.

- The standards are too geared to the engineering industry.

- The whole process of writing procedures, training staff, conducting internal audits, is expensive and time consuming.

- ISO 9000 does little to encourage statistical process control or continuous improvement.

The ISO 9000 approach

- Quality systems consist of three levels:

  - Level 1 - company quality manual.

  - Level 2 - procedures manual.

  - Level 3 - work instructions.

- ISO 9000 is the internationally recognized quality standard.

How quality awards seek to promote TQM

Points to make

1 Successful implementation of TQM depends on a number of factors.

These include: (a) a quality strategy; (b) top management support; (c) a steering group; (d) group-based improvement; (e) success being recognized; (f) appropriate training.

Sometimes TQM implementation is successful, but then its effect tails off. This can be avoided if: (a) TQM is not defined too narrowly; (b) all quality improvements are related to the organization's competitive priorities; (c) TQM is not used as a substitute for normal managerial leadership; (d) TQM is not 'bolted on'; (e) the hype is avoided; and (f) TQM is adapted to suit the organization.

Critics of TQM claim: (a) it can lead to a quality bureaucracy; (b) it can be incompatible with radical change programmes such as business process re-engineering; and (c) it is merely another example of management exploiting workers.

2 Various quality awards exist.

Quality awards are designed to recognize quality achievement and act as a spur for other organizations.

3 The best known quality awards include:

- The Deming Prize
- The Malcolm Baldrige National Quality Award
- The European Quality Award.

4 The Deming Prize.

Initially only Japanese companies could apply for the Deming Prize, but now the award is open to any company which has successfully applied 'company-wide quality control' based upon statistical quality control.

The Deming Prize is awarded on the basis of ten assessment categories: (a) policy and objectives; (b) organization and its operation; (c) education and its extension; (d) assembling and disseminating of information; (e) analysis; (f) standardization; (g) control; (h) quality assurance; (i) effects; and (j) future plans.

5 The Malcolm Baldridge National Quality Award.

The Malcolm Baldridge National Quality Award is awarded in America.

The examination categories are: (a) leadership; (b) information and analysis; (c) strategic quality planning; (d) human resource utilization; (e) quality assurance of products and services; (f) quality results; and (g) customer satisfaction.

6 The European Quality Award.

The European Quality Award is a self-assessment scheme, launched in 1992. It is based on a model which has nine elements: (a) customer satisfaction; (b) people (employee) satisfaction; (c) impact on society; achieved through (d) leadership; (e) driving policy and strategy; (f) people management; (g) resources; (h) processes; and all of which ultimately lead to (i) excellence in business results. The novelty of the European Quality Award is that each element can be classified either as a result or an enabler. Results describe what the company has achieved and is achieving. Enablers describe how the results are being achieved.

Quality awards

Leadership 10%	People management 9%	People satisfaction 9%
	Policy and strategy 8%	Processes 14%	Customer satisfaction 20%
	Resources 9%	Impact on society 6%

Business results 15%

← Enablers - 50% → ← Results - 50% →

The European Quality Award model

OHP113

CHAPTER 21

THE OPERATIONS CHALLENGE

Key questions
• Why should organizations have an operations strategy?
• How does ethics come into operations strategy?
• What are the main international issues faced by organizations formulating their operations strategies?
• How can operations strategies be creative?
• What influences the successful implementation of operations strategies?

Topics covered
• The challenges of operations strategy formulation.
• How the decisions resulting from operations strategies have an ethical dimension.
• Why operations strategies need to be considered from an international perspective.
• Why challenging the trade-off paradigm of operations involves creative operations strategies.
• How an implementation agenda is needed to put operations strategies into practice.

Summary
Why should organizations have an operations strategy?
• Because the evidence seems to show that an effective operations strategy helps organizations to compete more effectively. It does this by helping policies to be more coherent, helping to prioritize internal conflict and giving structure to the internal debate on which direction to choose.
• However, there are a number of difficulties in formulating successful operations strategies.
> Operations managers tend to be geographically dispersed;
> Operations managers operate in real time and so therefore need to manage the operation;
> Operations resources are difficult to change;
> Operations managers are often not in the habit of contributing to strategic change.
• Operations strategies can be classified into categories of generic strategies. One such classification distinguishes between caretaker strategies, marketeer strategies, reorganiser strategies and innovator strategies.

How do ethics come into operations strategy?
• Practically all decisions made by operations managers have some kind of ethical dimension. These ethical considerations affect one or more of the following groups:
> the operation's customers;
> the operation's staff;
> the operation's suppliers;
> the community in which the operation exists;
> the operation's shareholders and owners.
• Some companies make their ethical stance explicit through a statement of mission and values.

What are the main international issues faced by operations strategies?

• The first is how to configure their resources throughout the world. There are four configurations. These are:

Home country configuration;

Regional configuration;

Global co-ordinated configuration;

Combined regional and global co-ordinated configuration.

International operations need to address the problems of managing their operations across national boundaries. An issue here is how to balance competition and co-operation.

• Different regions in the world often develop different operations practices depending on the economic, social and political circumstances. However, some of these practices developed in one part of the world can be transferred (often in a modified form) to other parts of the world.

How can operations strategies be creative?

• One of the main concepts which helps to explain creativity in operations is that of the 'trade-off'. Originally theories of operations suggested that operations managers needed to merely manage the extent of trade-offs between performance objectives. More recently theories suggest that overcoming the long-term effects of trade-offs is a useful way of ensuring creativity in organizations.

What influences the successful implementation of operations strategies?

• Partly ensuring that any change is accompanied by a worked-through 'implementation agenda'. This will deal with such basic questions as:

When should the implementation start?

Where should the implementation start?

How fast should the implementation proceed?

How should the implementation programme be co-ordinated?

• In addition studies tend to show that successful implementations have top management support, are business driven, make technology decisions driven by the strategy itself, have changes which are integrated, invest in people as well as technology and manage technology as well as people.

The challenges of operations strategy formulation

Points to make

1 **It is important to distinguish between the content of an operations strategy and the process by which it is formulated.**
Content is the output of the operations strategy process. Content addresses the question - what is your operations strategy? Process addresses the question - how did you develop your operations strategy?

2 **Operations is complicated by the fact that it has many elements.**
Putting these together into a coherent whole so that they all help the business compete is a challenging task, but this is what we seek to do when formulating an operations strategy.

3 **What are the advantages of having an operations strategy?**
A formal operations strategy helps ensure that the policies adopted in the operations function fit together in a coherent manner. The strategy provides a framework for future decision making and gives the operations function direction.

4 **What are the difficulties in formulating an operations strategy?**
In addition to the complexity there are four particular problems that have to be faced. Operations managers are central to the strategy formulation process and yet within any organization they are likely to be scattered around the world. Operations managers operate in real time. They cannot afford to leave the operation unattended for long periods. Constraints on what is possible are inevitable given the nature of the operation's resources. The previous three items have been problems for years. Hence operations managers are not used to thinking strategically.

The challenge of operations strategy formulation

An operations strategy should be:

- Appropriate...

- Comprehensive...

- Coherent...

- Consistent over time...

OHP114

How operations strategies have an ethical dimension

Points to make

1 Ethics can be considered as the framework of moral behaviour which determines whether we judge a particular decision as being right or wrong.

2 **An operation's ethical stance impacts various groups.**
These groups include customers, staff, suppliers, the community and the shareholders.

3 **An operation's ethical stance is often summarized in a statement of vision, mission or values.**

4 **The ethical implications of operations strategies include:**
Product/service design - customer safety, recyclability of materials, energy consumption.

Network design - employment implications and environmental impact of location, employment implications of plant closure, employment implications of vertical integration.

Layout of facilities - staff safety, disabled customer access, energy efficiency.

Process technology - staff safety, waste and product disposal, noise pollution, fumes and emissions, repetitive/alienating work, energy efficiency.

Job design - staff safety, workplace stress, repetitive/alienating work, unsocial working hours, customer safety (in high contact operations).

Planning and control - priority given to each customer, materials utilization and wastage, unsocial working hours, workplace stress, restrictive organizational cultures.

Capacity planning and control - hire and fire employment policies, working hour fluctuations, unsocial working hours, service cover in emergencies, relationships with subcontractors, dumping of products below cost.

Inventory planning and control - price manipulation in restricted markets, energy management, warehouse safety, obsolescence and wastage.

Supply chain planning and control - honesty in supplier relationships, transparency of cost data, non-exploitation of developing country suppliers, prompt payment to suppliers, minimizing energy consumption in distribution, using recycled materials.

Quality planning and control - customer safety, staff safety, workplace stress, scrap and wastage of materials.

Failure prevention and recovery - environmental impact of process failures, customer safety, staff safety.

Operations strategies have an ethical dimension

- Product/service design - customer safety, recyclability of materials, energy consumption.

- Network design - employment implications and environmental impact of location.

- Layout of facilities - staff safety, disabled customer access.

- Process technology - staff safety, waste and product disposal, noise pollution, fumes and emissions.

- Job design - workplace stress, unsocial working hours.

- Capacity planning and control - employment policies.

- Inventory planning and control - price manipulation.

The international perspective

Points to make

1 Most operations buy from or sell to business overseas.
Hence operations strategies have to be international.

2 There are four basic decisions that need to be made regarding international operations strategies.
Where should the operations facilities be located?

How should the operations network be managed across national boundaries?

Should operations in different countries be allowed to develop their own way of doing business?

Should an operations practice which has been successful in one part of the world be transferred to another?

3 Where should the operations facilities be located?
- Home country configuration. This is by far the simplest option. Plants are located only in the operation's home country. Goods and services are exported or imported as appropriate.

- Regional configuration. The market is divided into regions. Each region is served by its own operation(s). This configuration is adopted if customers want speedy delivery and good after-sales service.

- Global co-ordinated configuration. Operations are located so that they can exploit particular advantages of sites or regions. Products and services are exported. This configuration requires central co-ordination.

- Combined regional and global co-ordinated configuration. The regions are reasonably autonomous, but certain products or services are still made in certain areas.

4 How should the operations network be managed across national boundaries?
International businesses encounter various problems caused by language, culture and the local environment. Having said this, a major advantage of being multinational is that the business can begin to develop a multi-cultural perspective, which helps it understand new markets and ways of working.

5 Should operations in different countries be allowed to develop their own way of doing business?
If left alone, operations will develop their own ways of doing things. The question is - is this desirable?

6 Should an operation's practice which has been successful in one part of the world be transferred to another?
This is a complex question, made more difficult by the fact that even if it is desirable, it is not always possible to transfer 'best practices'. While it is often relatively straightforward to transfer the technical aspects of a practice, implementation usually involves tailoring the practice so it suits the local environment.

International operations network configurations

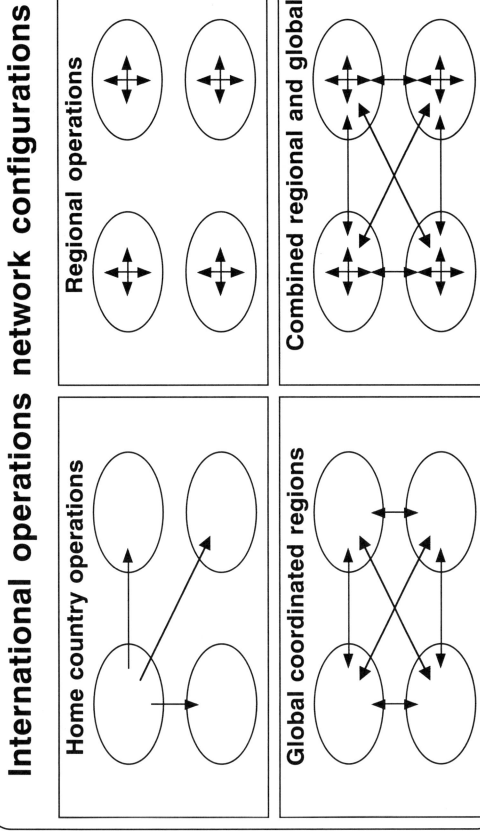

Home country operations

Regional operations

Global coordinated regions

Combined regional and global

OHP116

The trade-off relationship between performance objectives

Points to make

1 Procedures give structure to the strategy formulation process.
They do not provide the single best solution.

To create a 'good solution' you have to be innovative. Often this involves breaking free from the trade-off model of operations. The trade-off model holds that one way in which performance can be improved with regard to one objective is to trade-off performance with some other objective.

2 There is no such thing as a free lunch!
Wickham Skinner, one of the leading lights in operations strategy, said, 'Most managers will readily admit that there are compromises or trade-offs to be made in designing an aeroplane or truck. In the case of an aeroplane, trade-offs would involve matters such as cruising speed, take-off and landing distances, initial cost, maintenance, fuel consumption, passenger comfort and cargo or passenger capacity. For instance no one today can design a 500 passenger plane that can land on an aircraft carrier and also break the sound barrier. Much the same thing is true in manufacturing'.

3 Some firms appear to get the best of both worlds.
'Good food costs less at Sainsbury's'. In some industry sectors the model has changed. People appear to be able to overcome some trade-offs. Take, for example, cars. At one time high quality, reliable cars were inevitably expensive. Now, in most cases, even the cheapest cars are error-free.

4 What has changed?
Largely the attitude of operations managers. For years the prevailing wisdom was 'you can either have something that is good, or you can have something that is cheap'. Now people recognise that making things better does not have to cost more. In fact, making things better can reduce scrap, thereby reducing, rather than increasing, cost.

5 What has prompted this attitude change?
Pioneering Japanese firms have questioned the prevailing logic and over a period of time have been able to minimize the impact of various trade-offs. Others have seen this example and followed suit.

6 Over a period of time.
A key issue is timescale. It might be possible for a production manager to double volume overnight, but it would almost certainly be expensive. Over a six- or twelve-month period the story might be different because it might be possible to reconfigure the manufacturing system so that the worst of the trade-off could be overcome.

7 By attacking the pivot.
Imagine a supermarket. One of the key trade-offs is the number of tills operating versus the length of the queues. Customers do not like waiting. The supermarket does not want to have till operators standing idle. Hence there must be a trade-off. Some supermarkets have sought to overcome this problem by keeping a register of people who live locally and are willing to come to work at very short notice. Labour flexibility like this cannot be developed overnight, but once available, these 'extra' staff can be asked to come in as and when queues build up, thereby minimizing the impact of the trade-off.

Trade-off relationship between objectives

Performance objective 1

Performance objective 2

Improve performance by raising the pivot

An 'implementation agenda' is needed

Points to make

1 Operations strategies have to be implemented.
For this to happen an implementation agenda is needed. The implementation agenda should explore: (a) when to start; (b) where to start; (c) how fast to proceed; and (d) how to co-ordinate the implementation programme.

2 When to start?
The key rule is that implementation should not be started until all the issues on the implementation agenda have been addressed.

3 Where to start?
There are two schools of thought here. Some people argue that implementation should start where most impact will be felt. Others argue that implementation should start wherever success is most likely.

4 How fast to proceed?
The implementation programme can be continuous, breakthrough, or a combination of the two.

5 How to co-ordinate the implementation programme?
Implementation needs to be managed. It requires resources and the implementation programme should be reviewed as regular milestones are achieved.

6 Key elements to successful implementation can be identified.
These include:

- Top management support.

- Business driven.

- Strategy drives technology.

- Change strategies that are integrated.

- Investment in people as well as technology.

- Management of technology as well as people.

- Everybody on board.

- Clear explicit objectives.

- Time-framed project management.

An implementation agenda is needed

- When to start?

- Where to start?

- How fast to proceed?

- How to co-ordinate the implementation programme?